DARE TO LEARN

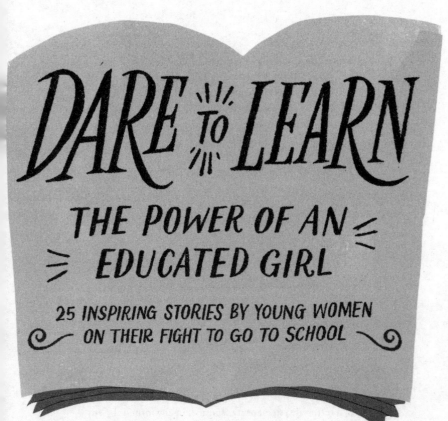

DARE TO LEARN

THE POWER OF AN EDUCATED GIRL

25 INSPIRING STORIES BY YOUNG WOMEN ON THEIR FIGHT TO GO TO SCHOOL

EDITED BY MALALA FUND
WITH A FOREWORD BY
MALALA YOUSAFZAI,
WINNER OF THE NOBEL PEACE PRIZE

HarperCollins *Publishers* India

First published in India by HarperCollins *Publishers* 2022
4th Floor, Tower A, Building No. 10, Phase II, DLF Cyber City,
Gurugram, Haryana – 122002
www.harpercollins.co.in

2 4 6 8 10 9 7 5 3 1

P-ISBN: 978-93-5489-560-9
E-ISBN: 978-93-5489-580-7

Typeset in 12/16.4 Adobe Garamond at
Manipal Technologies Limited, Manipal

Printed and bound at
Thomson Press (India) Ltd

This book is produced from independently certified FSC® paper
to ensure responsible forest management.

Contents

Foreword
by
Malala Yousafzai

I AM often asked to share my advice for girls on how to fight for their rights, but I don't think they need it.

In every community, in every country, girls are already speaking out. They're challenging injustice, confronting gender discrimination and overcoming obstacles to go to school.

These girls don't need my advice on how to fight for their rights because they're already fighting. What I can do is help amplify their voices.

In this book, you'll hear from twenty-five young women from around the world who have faced barriers to their education. In their own words, they will tell you about their journeys—their ideas, their setbacks and their triumphs. They're sharing the most challenging moments of their lives because they understand the power of their stories to create change, something I discovered when I started speaking out.

I was eleven years old when I first shared my story.

On an anonymous blog for the BBC, I wrote how the Taliban banned girls from going to school in my hometown of Swat Valley, Pakistan. How the sound of machine guns would wake me up at night. How I missed having picnics in the green hills of Swat Valley.

At the time, I just wanted to continue my education and help other girls in my community do the same. I didn't have the resources or influence to create change, I only had my voice. So that's what I used. I hoped that at least one person would listen to my story and would want to support my fight. I could never have imagined that people around the world would hear my words, that my call for education and equality would grow into a global movement.

A lot has changed in my life since then, but my mission—to ensure that no girl is denied her right to education—remains the same. Currently, nearly 130 million girls are out of school and the consequences of the Covid-19 pandemic could prevent another 20 million girls from continuing their education. With my organization, Malala Fund, I am fighting to break down the barriers preventing girls around the world from going to school.

Whether we're training girls to speak out through our Girl Programme, investing in the work of local education advocates with our Education Champion Network or advocating to hold leaders accountable to their commitments, girls' voices are at the centre of everything that Malala Fund does. I might have more resources and influence now than when I first started speaking out—but I'll never forget that girls who face the greatest education challenges often have the least visibility and that their voices need to be part of the solution.

I wanted to give girls around the world a platform to tell their stories, just like I had. Too often, leaders ignore the experiences of young women when making decisions about our future. But the world needs to hear from us. People at every level of power—from classrooms and boardrooms to the offices of presidents and prime ministers—need to hear from girls about the challenges we face and the changes we want to see. I created Assembly, Malala Fund's digital publication and newsletter, to give every girl that opportunity.

Assembly is a place where girls can tell their stories. From challenging gender discrimination in their communities and weighing in on the importance of girls in STEM to sharing about the companies and advocacy campaigns they're creating—Assembly contributors sound off on the issues and topics that matter to them. Through essays, poems, illustrations, photos, videos and more, Assembly provides a look into girlhood around the world through the eyes of girls.

Assembly is also a network of peers that girls can turn to for inspiration. Readers can discover ideas for their own advocacy, learn about the challenges that girls in different countries face or find solace in knowing they're not alone in fighting for education and equality. It's a meeting place for girls around the world and the kind of resource I wish I had when I first began speaking out.

Since we launched Assembly in July 2018, we've published content about girls and young women from over a hundred countries in over twenty-six languages. And now we're reaching even more readers through this book.

This anthology features chapters from twenty-five Assembly contributors. You'll learn about young women from Brazil, Canada, Ethiopia, India, Iraq, Morocco, Nigeria, Pakistan, Syria, Uganda, the United Kingdom (UK), the United States (US), and Venezuela who have struggled to go to school. The challenges these young women face vary between communities and countries, but one factor is constant in every story: they know that education is their best hope for a brighter tomorrow.

After reading these pages, you will learn why more than 130 million girls are out of school—and how we can address these issues. Aisha Mustapha from Nigeria writes about the piercing fear of fleeing Boko Haram and finding her way back to school after years of displacement. Azka Athar explains the gender discrimination that prevents Pakistani girls from pursuing careers in STEM—and how she challenged those beliefs by leading an all-female team of students in building a race car. And Tabitha Willis describes the racism Black students like her experience in American public schools and how teachers can better support students of colour.

Many of the girls in this book are from India, where nearly 40 per cent of girls from ages fifteen to eighteen are out of school. From Vandana Bharti, you will learn how high tuition fees keep the most marginalized girls from learning and how she is advocating for laws to help change that. Anoyara Khatun shares how she had to start working at the age of twelve to support her family—and how now she's rescuing other children from child labour. And Anjeli describes travelling long distances from her tea plantation to school because she knows education is the best way to secure her future.

To each of the young women who contributed to this book, I want to say thank you. Gender discrimination, conflict, poverty, racism, displacement and more may have disrupted your lives but you are refusing to let the challenges you've faced define your future. In sharing your story, you are paving the way for the next generation of girls and ensuring they don't have to work as hard as we did to go to school. In contributing to this book, you are showing that your courage is stronger than your fear.

I also want to acknowledge that many of the girls featured in this book are able to go to school thanks to the support of Malala Fund's Education Champions. These local educators and activists identify threats to girls' education in their communities and develop solutions. With Malala Fund's investment, our Education Champions are scaling their efforts and leveraging their collective power to make it easier for all girls to learn. In the fight to see every girl in school, we're so lucky to have allies like you.

And to our readers, I hope you are reminded of what girls and women can accomplish when we are given the tools to learn and lead. If you are a parent, teacher or community leader, I hope that you are motivated to examine the barriers preventing girls in your community from reaching their full potential and to explore how you can help break those down.

And if you are a young woman reading this book, I hope you see yourself and your life reflected in these pages and that you remember your capacity to create change. When I started my movement for girls' education, I didn't know if anyone would listen to an eleven-year-old, but I wanted people everywhere to know what was happening to my community and our schools. It was then that I learned that my story has power—and I want you to know that yours does too. This book celebrates twenty-five girls' voices, but we need to hear more.

I hope to hear your story next.

Note from Malala Fund

MALALA began speaking out for girls' education at the age of eleven and she continues her campaign today through her organization, Malala Fund. She created Assembly, Malala Fund's digital publication and newsletter, to help other young women tell their stories, just like she did.

Assembly is a platform for young women's voices—and a source of ideas and inspiration in their fight for education and equality.

Put together by Tess Thomas, the editor of Assembly, *Dare to Learn* features twenty-five essays by Assembly contributors from around the world on their fight to go to school. With stories from Brazil, Canada, Ethiopia, India, Iraq, Morocco, Nigeria,

Pakistan, Syria, Uganda, the UK, the US, and Venezuela, this book highlights how young women are confronting the barriers preventing them from learning and working to make our world a more equal place.

To read more, you can visit assembly.malala.org

1

Vandana Bharti

INDIA

WHEN I was fourteen years old, I had a tough choice to make: keep going to school or help provide for my family by working during school hours.

My family's financial situation was not good at the time. My father has gone to school and is literate, unlike most other people in our village in Kushinagar district. However, despite being a graduate, he was having trouble getting a job. He needed me to leave school to help my mother in the fields and provide for my family. To meet family obligations, I had no choice but to drop out. I understood my family needed me, but I was very sad about leaving school and cried a lot. I loved school and was a good student. I was extremely upset on my last day in class, I thought my dreams would never be fulfilled.

My story isn't unique. In my village, there isn't a government school or free education beyond eighth grade, so most girls end up as child labourers or child brides and face a life of endless exploitation. Currently, India's Right to Education Act, 2009, only guarantees free and compulsory schooling for children up to the age of fourteen. Once we turn fourteen and complete eighth grade, our access to free education ends. Almost 40 per cent of girls in India between the ages of fifteen to eighteen are not in school.

For two years, I worked with my mother in the fields, fulfilling my responsibility to help her and our family. I have two brothers and two sisters. They too had to drop out of school early due to financial constraints. However, even though we have all experienced these challenges, my sisters and I are not treated the same as our brothers. We're not considered at par with them. In our community, boys get more freedom to do things than girls; while we are forced to do household work. In fact, it's a practice to serve food to girls only after the boys have been served. Families don't want to invest in educating their daughters because after they grow up and get married, they move away to live with their in-laws. So what's the point in it?

A significant part of the issue is that most people in my Dalit community aren't educated and don't understand the importance of going to school. Most people aren't even aware of their basic rights. There's not enough land for farming, so many people have to do daily wage work—including women and children. Parents don't have enough time to nurture their children and men often waste their wages on liquor. However, I know the importance of educating girls. It is only by going to school, developing our mind and learning about our rights that we can stand on our own feet and make a difference in society.

Those two years when I was working and not studying were hard for me, but thankfully I got a second chance. Samudaik Kalyan Evam Vikas Sansthan (SKVS) is a Malala Fund-supported organization that works to help Dalit and Muslim girls in my community go to school. They did a survey and found that many children in my village—especially girls—are out of school. They formed a mothers' group, Mahila Sangathan, which my mother joined. It was then that social workers from SKVS came to my parents and explained to them that letting me continue my education would lead to my development and that of our society. They explained that education is a right and that the people in our community would have a better life if all the girls went to school. They persuaded my parents to let me continue my education.

That's when I was able to re-enrol in tenth grade. I was so happy. I finally felt like I was going to be able to achieve my dreams. However, I still faced many challenges as I struggled to cover my school expenses. I needed to work after school and on weekends to be able to pay for my admission fee and supplies. I hate working in the fields, but there's no other option for me.

Since there isn't a closer school, I have to walk 4 km each way to the nearest one. It is 8 km of walking every day, which doesn't leave me with any time to complete my homework. It'd be easier if I had a bicycle, but my father uses our bicycle to go to his new job at the brick kiln. I also face other challenges like making new friends after being out of school for so long, adjusting again to being in a classroom with teachers, and comments from boys as I walk to school alone. My parents often worry about me returning home so late. But I have promised myself that regardless of these barriers, I will focus on completing my studies.

Even though I'm back in school, I'll never forget what it was like to drop out and to fear that my dreams for the future might never come true. I almost lost my right to education—and I don't wish to see any more of my sisters lose theirs. That's why I'm also working on making it easier for other girls in my community and across India to be able to go to school. In 2020, I started an online petition to ask our Union Human Resource Development Minister Ramesh Pokhriyal and Finance Minister Nirmala Sitharaman to increase the contribution to education through public resources so that all children can receive free education up to the higher secondary level.

Over 85,000 people have signed the petition to date. Unfortunately, the Union Budget 2021-22 came as a big disappointment as it failed to allocate the required amount to undo the impact of the Covid-19 pandemic. Yet again, the budget didn't allocate enough of the GDP to education. This neglect will adversely impact children, particularly those from poor, marginalized communities and also girls, like me, adding to the already increasing number of out-of-school children in India.

This couldn't have come at a worse time. Due to the Covid-19 pandemic and the extended school closure, students have lost out on a lot of learning. Many children from marginalized communities were unable to access online education during school closure and instead they had to focus on household chores. The possibility of these children dropping out of the education system looms large.

There is an urgent need for the government to invest in education to boost the economic growth of the country. Many young girls like me depend on this for our future.

My life is so much better now that I'm back in school. My favourite subject is sociology because it teaches me about our society and what we can do to improve it. I get to participate in sports with my friends (I recently came in first in a 100-metre race and won a medal!), study, learn and also participate in cultural programmes. I want to become a police officer when I'm older to help women and girls get justice and to reduce corruption. The only way this dream will come true is if I am able to finish my education. Whenever I see other girls being forced out of school, the first thought that comes to my mind is that the girl won't be able to achieve her dream. It's not only her loss, but also her community's and her family's loss. That's what hurts me the most.

Other girls in my community are now pursuing education inspired by my example. It makes me so happy to have other girls join me in education and I feel proud to see that parents are sending their girls to school. But families can't address these issues alone. We need government support.

The government needs to invest more in girls' education so that there are more schools for girls to attend and poorer families don't have to pay so much for school fees and supplies. Many girls don't go to high school or inter-college in my village because it's too far and families consider it too dangerous to send their daughters to a school outside the village when there is no safe transportation. Girls have been molested and harassed by boys while walking or cycling to a school far from home.

If there were a government high school or inter-college near my village, this problem would be eliminated. The only way to make sure all girls have access to education is by ensuring the extension of the Right to Education Act up to higher secondary level and also that more money is spent by the government to build secondary schools in every village.

A recent study conducted in my village and in other places to assess the impact of the Covid-19 pandemic found that most children were unsure about whether they will return to school—37 per cent of them did not answer the question or said that they didn't know, pointing to high uncertainties of education. The government needs to operationalize the National Education Policy's Gender Inclusion Fund (as also the Inclusion Fund for other marginalized groups) to support school reopening and re-enrolment in the immediate term and ensure that secondary education is made free for all children by extension of the Right to Education Act for up to eighteen years of age.

If the government fulfils its promise of allocating 6 per cent of the GDP on education, there could be a secondary school in villages like mine. Thousands of girls like me who have missed out on their education because of the Covid-19 pandemic would be able to return to school and learn the skills that can contribute to the development of our nation.

My future seemed bleak because of the lack of government investment in girls' education. It's time our leaders prioritized our future so that no other girl has to choose between going to school and providing for her family.

2
Nibras Basitkey
IRAQ

WHEN I was a child, the first scene I would wake up to in the mornings was the tiny mountains of Sreshka in northern Iraq. They are more like big hills, but to my child's mind, it carried all the splendour and grandeur of mountains. In our village, there was one single road that led to the outside world, but the farmers were more content to spend their days on the fields that they lovingly tended to. Most of the villagers felt no need to venture outside as they were content with the life they had built there.

Sreshka was a very beautiful and peaceful place. Our minds were not burdened with the trivial worries of the outside world. We were satisfied with the world we had created: our houses, our food, our farms. Everything we used and consumed was a product of our labour, and as such, a product of our love and pride. We all had an established routine of waking up, going to work on the farm, eating and then gathering with the community.

Although it was such a loving community, there is so much I now miss about Sreshka, I knew from an early age that I didn't share the same mindset as most of my community—particularly in terms of beliefs towards girls' education and the role of women in society. Every day I would go to my high school to see an empty chair where my friend used to be and feel the familiar sinking feeling in my stomach knowing that she had dropped out to get married.

The practice of marrying girls off at a young age is accepted without question in the community. The teachers at the school also continue teaching even after girl students drop out as though nothing is wrong. Some families don't believe in the value of girls' education, while others prefer to invest in their sons rather than daughters because they see no future for their girls. For families scrimping and pinching to make ends meet, they would rather use what little resources they have to educate their sons, who are considered as assets, as opposed to their daughters, who were seen more as liabilities.

Unfortunately, most girls have bought into the narrative that their role in life is limited to that of a wife and within the four walls of the house, and thus, are willing to drop out of school to get married. These girls are surrounded by people drilling in their head that their sole responsibility is to cook, clean and raise children. And most have accepted this without question.

The one thing that set me apart from other girls in my village was my thirst for knowledge, and my goal to complete high school. I aspired for greater things in life and was lucky to have a father who supported my ambitions. My dad was one of the few people in our community who broke the mould of the world he was used to and left Sreshka to work basic jobs in Baghdad. The city of Baghdad presented my father with the image of a world where women were successful professionals and could be whatever they aspired to be.

He realized that there were opportunities for me out in the world but not in the village, where conservative mindsets continued to impede women's progress. He saw a future for me that was not limited to the household and extended beyond the boundaries of what people at the village thought was possible for women. I wanted that future as well; I wanted to pave the way for other girls to follow my example and realize that they did not have to limit themselves to being a wife and mother. I wanted to evoke a sense of awe and respect when I walked into a room. I wanted to be able to converse with men about current events and local issues. The sad reality was that there was no place for a woman in these conversations in my village. The conversation among most of the girls revolved around their dolma recipes, who asked for Katarine's hand in marriage, and complaining about their lazy siblings not helping around the house.

All I wanted to talk about was the problems in our community, and what we could do to tackle those. I wanted to make a difference and contribute to society because I knew I had the potential. And I knew that education was the key to be able to do that.

My motivation was not purely driven by self-interest, but by an overall goal to create a future where all the girls could be educated and inspired to follow their dreams. I knew that if one girl could break through and graduate high school, she would pave the way for others. So, I focused on school and on being the best student I could be. If I graduated, got a job and helped support my family, then other families might also see the value of educating their daughters.

My favourite subject in school was maths. To most students, maths is a subject that they want to steer clear of. But to me, each mathematical problem served as an embodiment of a problem in my own life. If I could successfully solve for 'x', why would I not be able to solve the problems of child marriage and girls' education in my own community?

My educational journey was not without obstacles. I faced a lot of challenges, such as the fact that though my books were written in Kurdish, most of the teachers only spoke in Arabic. However, what I was most grateful for was that as long as I was still in school I had the opportunity to learn.

One day, in 2014, my life in Sreshka came crashing down. I had just finished high school and was celebrating the title of the 'student of the year' for achieving the highest GPA. As I was walking home, I saw crowds of people fleeing, screaming and children crying. The terrorist organization ISIS had taken over Mosul, a city only thirty minutes away from Sreshka.

Growing up near a war zone, you always live in the fear of the worst happening. We knew when ISIS invaded Syria, the border wasn't secure and that it wouldn't be long before they came for us. We were especially at risk as a minority; ISIS had made it very clear that Yazidis like us were the target. But we didn't know it would happen as fast as it did. We didn't know that ISIS would seize the entire city of Mosul in a span of just two hours.

After they took Mosul, Christians and other religious minorities fled the city. They poured into our village, desperately heading for the mountains in the north. It was then that we realized that we had to leave as well before it was too late.

My friends started running to find their families, fearing that they would be left behind. Drones were flying above us. Peshmerga fighters, who are Kurdish forces, were moving in, pushed back by the ISIS advance. I don't remember how I got to my house. My family only had time to grab our passports and IDs. Twelve people piled into our small car, many climbed on the roof. A lot of other people just ran.

I was fifteen years old at the time. My siblings were even younger. I remember the feeling of terror running through my veins. I tried to make sense of my world as it now stood. Was I now a refugee in my own home? It felt like the world was ending. There were people everywhere, everyone was running, everything was in a state of chaos. The events that followed our escape are pretty much a blur now because there was so much happening around me. It was overwhelming and my mind had shut down.

My family of eight ended up in Erbil, a Kurdish city about 120 km away from Sreshka. We were there for about three months, unsure about whether we would be able to return. I tried to enrol in school there, but they would not accept me without a signed transcript. My father and I had to return to our old village—from where ISIS was now only 4 km away—so that the principal could sign my transcript. At the top of the mountain, I could see the

ISIS flags and its members. It was the most terrifying moment in my life. But even that bone-chilling fear could not stop me. All my life I have fought to get educated, and even the fear of ISIS could not stop me.

My father and I put our lives at risk that day, when we went back to get that transcript. We put our lives on the line because I knew that only by going to school would I have a brighter future. I didn't want household chores to be my only duty as it had always been for other women in my community. I wanted to be able to do anything a boy would do. I wanted a good education because I had dreams and goals—and I didn't want ISIS stopping me. I didn't want my status as a refugee coming in my way.

I returned to Erbil and began school again. On my first day there, I saw over five hundred girls heading into the school building and got very excited. Attitude towards girls' education was different there. I didn't have to face discrimination anymore because of my gender, like it had been in my village. It was normal for girls to go to school there. I was ready for my education to be easy.

But from the moment I walked into my new school, it wasn't easy. The Kurdish dialect used there was different and I was also one of the few girls in the school not wearing a head cover. I had assumed people would be understanding because they knew I belonged to a different religion. They were aware that ISIS was targeting Yazidis like me, but they didn't seem to show any empathy. The school officials wouldn't use my name, they referred to me as the 'Yazidi girl'.

Students and teachers alike made derogatory comments about Yazidis. I was taunted and harassed. It seemed the only difference between the school and the terror of ISIS was that my classmates didn't have weapons, although it felt like they did. They were using their words as weapons every single day, even in the classroom.

I couldn't and still can't understand the hate. I came from a Kurdish territory and always identified as a Kurd, much like the people in Erbil. The only difference between us was our religion, and I thought they would accept me despite that. But that did not happen.

Yet I persevered, working hard, ignoring people's comments and focusing only on getting an education and good grades. I was grateful to be able to go to school because most of my former classmates from my old village did not make it to a safe place where they could continue their education.

Since my father worked with the US Army, we received continuous threats from terrorist groups in Iraq. That was when my family petitioned to move to the US. It was a joy-filled moment when I received my visa. My dreams had come true—I was leaving a place of war and hate. I arrived in a place where people would smile at you without even knowing you.

The first day of school in the US was a magical moment for me. I was in a world where girls and boys studied alongside each other. There was a world of books to explore and choose from. For once in my life, no one asked me what my religion was.

At that point, I didn't speak English. This was a major challenge for me because I felt like I was starting from scratch all over again. I felt all my struggles to get educated and my hard work in Iraq had been for nothing. I told my family that I couldn't do it and that I wanted to quit. I didn't have the strength left in me to fight anymore. Why did I have to struggle so much to get an education? Why did I have to chase what seemed so easy for everyone else?

I was almost off the tipping point and thought that maybe it was not meant to be. But my father helped rally my spirit and told me that the US was the place where I was going to succeed, the place where I could be whoever I wanted to be. He reminded me that a lot of other refugee girls were still in camps and didn't have the same opportunities as me. I had to do this for myself and for them.

I focused on vocabulary first. I took my dad's advice to learn ten words every day, telling him the new words I had learnt when he picked me up from school. I knew if my English-speaking classmates studied for one hour, I would need to study for two. I researched strategies to improve my English, like reading out loud and writing journal entries every day. By the end of the year, I had graduated from my English support classes. I finally felt that I had overcome my challenges and that high school graduation was well within my reach.

I joined the debate team to further improve my English. In the first competition I participated in, I don't think the judges understood any of what I spoke in my mixed Arabic, Kurdish and English. But with constant practice, I improved. By the end of the year, I was able to communicate as well as the Americans on my team and finally the judges could understand what side I was arguing for! And then my debate partner and I made it to the quarterfinals of the Nebraska State Debate Championship.

The day of my graduation was very emotional. I had never thought I'll be able to complete high school. The journey was so hard for me, while it seemed so easy for everyone else. But I had made it. That whole day I thought about my village, how much I had changed and how far I had come. I gave the commencement speech at the ceremony. A few minutes before walking on stage, I asked my best friend, Mahsa, to pinch me just to make sure it was not all just a dream.

In my speech, I shared the story of what had brought me to that stage and how my parents used to tell my siblings and I that education is 'the candle that lights the world'. Both my parents were denied the right to learn. My father's parents forced him to drop out of school to work on a farm. My mother has only studied till the second grade because her parents did not see a future for girl students. I told my classmates to take their light and brighten the world with their education. Then I turned my tassel, threw my cap in the air and became the first person from my family to graduate high school and, later, the first one to attend college.

After I finished my speech, I looked at my fellow students and wished that the girls back in my village were there too. That they too could have had the opportunity to complete their high school education. But instead of going to college as many of us were, they were now grappling with the responsibility of having and caring for children before they were ready. Whether I'm heading to class or getting ready to speak at the United Nations, those girls are always on my mind. They will always be on my mind until every girl in the world gets the opportunity to go to school and realize her full potential.

All my life I have known I had potential. But as a girl in my village, I was told I didn't have any. However, after graduating and starting my degree at university, I felt like the world was finally seeing the potential I always saw in myself. It was then that I began my activism for girls' education. I believe that if my words can convince even one parent to educate their daughter; if my story can help even one girl break barriers and achieve what I did, then my entire journey of fighting for girls' education will be worth it.

3

Aisha Mustapha

NIGERIA

M Y first experience with Boko Haram happened when I was nine years old and living in Konduga, a town in northeastern Nigeria, with my parents.

One day, my sister and I had gone to a small community nearby called Dalori for a wedding. We were having fun with our family and friends. Everyone was so excited about the wedding and had travelled far to be there. I was really enjoying meeting relatives I had never met before. Everyone was surprised at how much I had grown up. I was sitting and chatting with my family members from another area of the state when suddenly my uncle came into the compound looking very anxious. He cautioned us to remain indoors as some strange faces were noticed in the town. They were suspected to be members of the Boko Haram sect.

I had heard stories of Boko Haram attacks in Maiduguri, the state capital. Most of our relatives who lived there had to move to our villages. I had heard gunshots and bomb blasts from a distance earlier, but never close to me. We thought it was a problem for people living in the city. We didn't know it would also affect us.

We spent a sleepless night. My whole family was there so I was scared that all of us would be killed if there was an attack and that we would lose everyone. But nothing happened that night. The next morning, my aunty sent my younger sister and I to the roadside to buy some onions and condiments so that she could prepare breakfast for the family that morning. On our way back, we heard a bomb blast and gun shots all over the town. Trapped by the attack, we could not go back to our house.

We managed to run into the house nearest to us, which was a scholar's house, only to find him slaughtered in cold blood. We got scared and joined other people running for dear lives. We pushed our way back to our family's house somehow but by the time we got there, everyone else had already fled. The house was empty. We were separated from our family.

I was afraid I'll never see my family again, but we had to find safety first. We kept running and at the border of the town we met a young woman who offered help by leading us in a nearby town called Bama. She had seen that we were all alone and so young, and offered to help us. She was older than us, but not too old. We decided it would be safest for us to follow her. I'm so glad we did. For the next year, she became our foster mother.

The three of us journeyed for a day and spent a night hiding in the bushes. We were worried about men following us. We didn't sleep at all so that we could keep a lookout. We made it to Bama the following morning and spent about a week there before Boko Haram arrived there too and then even Bama wasn't safe. We ran away farther to Bank, a border town to Cameroon. Boko Haram was invading almost every part of that border, so when Bank also seemed unsafe, we crossed the border into Cameroon.

There's a lot I can't remember now from the time my sister, our foster mother and I spent running. What I do remember is that I kept thinking if it was the last day of my life. My head was ringing from constantly worrying about my safety and what had happened to my family. I wondered if my mother had survived the attack and how we'd ever be able to reunite with her.

Once we were in Cameroon, the three of us found solace as internally displaced peoples (IDPs). We lived in a former school that was converted into a camp for people like us who had to flee for our lives. Our foster mother was very kind to us. But she struggled to get enough food for us because resources were so scarce. Every day she'd go out and try to find jobs or labour she could do for money so that she could get food for us. Most of the time she was able to provide us two meals a day. And if she wasn't able to get enough food for all of us, she'd go hungry so that we could eat.

We spent nearly a year in Cameroon. I wasn't enrolled in school there because we were trying to survive there first. I helped our foster mother get firewood so that we could cook our food. If we couldn't get any firewood, I would search for animal dung so that we could burn that instead.

One day, I was sent to fetch water. I was carrying some buckets when I looked ahead of me and saw my brother! I started to shout and scream, I was so excited. I couldn't believe he was standing right before me. We started hugging, shouting and celebrating with each other. Although I hadn't known, my brother had escaped through Bama when our village was attacked. He told me that our mother had escaped towards Maiduguri during the attack in Dalori, while he had escaped with our grandmother to Cameroon like me.

I brought him immediately to my sister and foster mother. It was so joyful. The four of us then decided to try to return to Nigeria, so we boarded a bus provided by the government to help IDPs like us return. We couldn't go directly to Maiduguri because it wasn't still safe, so we went through Cameroon and then through Mubi in Adamawa state. It took us ten days to make that journey. The bus couldn't move very fast because of the roads. The rainy season made it really muddy and we often had to wait for tractors to pull us through difficult stretches. For food, we had to rely on the charity of the villages we passed or local governments. It was very hard.

When we finally arrived in Maiduguri, it had been a full year since the first attack in Dalori. A year that I spent apart from my mother. When we finally saw her again in Maiduguri, it was the best feeling in the world. I was so happy. We all shouted and cried. My mom hugged the woman who took care of us and they both shed tears of joy. My foster mother was also able to reunite with her husband.

From there on, we went to various camps of our local government. Our culture does not support a woman who heads a house. Since we were a woman-headed family, a friend of my father who was also an IDP from our village offered us a place to stay under his custody. It was then that we enrolled in Pompomari Primary School and completed our sixth grade. But my mother was struggling to pay for our education. As my brother is the only man of the house, the expectation is that he will one day shoulder my father's responsibility. Where I come from, the tradition is to put men and boys first. Therefore, my sister and I could not continue our education so that our brother could study further.

It was hard to watch him go to school while we stayed at home. Fortunately for me, Hallmark Leadership Initiative, an organization supported by Malala Fund, had a project where a coalition of community members identifies out-of-school girls and connects them with Hallmark Leadership Initiative so that they can be helped. The coalition was aware my sister and I were out of school, so the Hallmark Leadership Initiative told us they would be enrolling us back to school and supporting us with books, school shoes and uniforms. I could not believe it. I was back in school and my future was bright again.

I have recently completed my junior secondary, and now I'm getting ready for senior secondary school. My favourite subjects in school are English and mathematics. In my community, people who speak English are seen as wise. People respect you when you speak English and I want that respect too. I love mathematics because I know it's an essential subject for achieving my dream of becoming a nurse and supporting women in my community. I saw a pregnant woman in Dalori die due to lack of medical attention while delivering during a Boko Haram attack. I don't want that to happen to anyone else. I wouldn't have been able to get through my displacement if I hadn't been supported by people like my foster mother. It's because of that support that I want to learn and be able to support other girls like me in my community.

4

Angelina Tropper

CANADA

BEFORE I learnt about my attention deficit hyperactivity disorder (ADHD) and learning disability, school was a struggle. My teachers made assumptions about me and some other kids would even bully me. I would be assigned group projects and not be able to understand something everyone else seemed to get. My classmates would get very frustrated with me. Some of them would purposefully make me feel bad for not understanding. They would say things like 'I don't get why you don't get what everyone else does!' or 'How do you still not understand this even with the extra help from the teachers?' Some teachers too would immediately get frustrated with me when I wouldn't turn in my work on time. They would assume I was just being lazy when in fact the truth was that I would be up all night trying to finish just the first few questions. These experiences discouraged me a lot. They made me afraid to ask questions and made me uncertain about school in general.

Due to this attitude of my teachers and classmates, I became afraid of going to school. I didn't want to get embarrassed when reading out aloud or solving math problems on the board. Math was the toughest subject for me. The lesson would go by fast and I wouldn't be able to understand a single thing, especially when we were learning something new. Every morning we had to write tests on multiplication tables and our teachers timed us. Those made me nervous from the start. Even though I was able to improve on those tests through a lot of practice, I never got to 90 or above in under two minutes like everyone else did by the second month. I was always really embarrassed when I had to say my marks out loud to the entire class because everyone else would get high marks, and then there would be me getting 30 or 40 out of 100 multiplication questions. I tried to hide it as much as I could.

Observing all my classmates succeeding at something when I kept failing—even when I would spend endless hours studying—made me frustrated and discouraged. Hearing other kids say they didn't study or didn't even have to try hard to complete these math tests made me not want to try anymore. Those comments hit me the most and that's when I started losing faith in myself. I believed that no matter how much I tried, I wouldn't be as good as the other kids in my class. I felt discouraged, embarrassed, different, and left out because I always had to put in more effort than all my friends. It didn't matter how hard I worked—it was never enough.

Homework, that was supposed to take only twenty minutes, would take me over two hours—especially math. I would just sit there and not be able to understand anything. It was as if I was stuck underneath a pile of rocks and couldn't get out. When it came to reading out aloud or copying from the board, it was especially hard. For many students, it is probably the easiest thing to just copy something, but for me it isn't. It is difficult for me to focus on lines when I am reading and I often skip letters, words or even sentences. Some of my friends would say that they could read a book in one day or a week. But it took me many weeks or even months to do the same. This really frustrated me as I love books. My favourite genre is fantasy because it makes me feel like I'm escaping the real world. When I was having such a tough time in school, fantasy books would transport me to a world where all my problems disappeared and I could experience everything the story offered. The characters would go through trying times too, and I could relate to them. Reading books always made me feel better, even if it took me an eternity to finish them. I would always take my time to really understand the book and all the meaning behind it. Whenever I read for fun, I loved the fact that I didn't have any deadline from a teacher that I needed to finish it by. I could just read.

But my love for books didn't translate to love for school. In the beginning, my parents and teachers didn't really notice the problems I was facing because my overall grades were never that bad. But soon my parents began to lose their patience with me at home. They wouldn't believe me when I told them that I did study or read my homework. I would think to myself, 'Why can't

I read a book that fast or do my homework that quickly? Why is it so hard for me to understand or remember things?'

I started getting anxious, being temperamental and was not able to sleep at night. Before going to sleep at night, I would think about how in the morning I will have to go back to school and face all my problems. My brain wouldn't stop thinking. I felt so much pressure to perform better, but I just couldn't. I remember I used to pray that my parents forget to wake me up and just leave me behind at home so that I don't have to go to school. I was so sad, scared and anxious. Those feelings were so daunting that I felt like they were suffocating me. It was so difficult at times that it literally took my breath away. I would get such bad anxiety attacks that it would be difficult to breathe at times. It was particularly bad before exams.

In the mornings, I would have a very bad attitude towards my parents. Not only was I exhausted from being up all night, but I was also very anxious about going to school. I would blame them in my head for sending me to school. I was desperate to tell them what I was going through, but I was afraid they wouldn't understand. I couldn't understand myself as to why I wasn't doing better even when I was trying so hard. Every time I came home from school I would be in a bad mood as soon as 'school' came up in a conversation. I knew I would have to be up till late again to finish my homework. I felt very misunderstood by everyone, especially my parents. They didn't understand at the time that I was really struggling with school. They thought I lacked discipline or was just being lazy.

One day, my teacher talked to my parents about how I was struggling with my writing, my grades were dropping and that she had noticed certain patterns in my behaviour. She told my parents that I should take an assessment to see if I had any learning challenges. My parents listened to her. The test was actually a lot of fun and the people there were very nice. When I got the results, I was diagnosed with a learning disability and ADHD.

I was so relieved with my diagnosis because until then I really thought that there was something wrong with me and that I wasn't smart. It felt like a rock had been lifted off my back. The doctors explained to me that I had actually done well in the tests and that I was really smart, but my brain was just wired differently. They said that I would have to just find different ways of learning and that with time I would know exactly how to do that.

It's been five and a half years since my diagnosis. Since then, I've learned some tools that help me both in the classroom and at home. One is to meditate before I go to sleep at night and in the mornings, even if it is just for five minutes. In those five minutes, I forget the stress. It can get very busy and loud during the day. At times it can be very overwhelming. I find that there are so many things my brain has to take in, especially in school. Meditation helps me control my breathing and anxiety.

I also got a tutor who specialized in teaching kids with learning disabilities. She taught me that if I ask someone to read my history or social studies chapters out loud to me, my brain can focus on just listening and I can pay 100 per cent attention that way. Once I started doing that, I was able to easily answer the questions in my homework. Instead of writing the answers out myself, my tutor showed me a tool on Google where I could just speak to my computer and it would write everything for me.

It has made things much easier for me. But since I love writing I still try to write the answers out first and then just use spell and grammar checks. This has made a huge difference. It has shown me and proved to everyone else that I do know the answers to problems and questions I have to do for school.

I also write in my agenda not just what I have to do for homework, but things I can look forward to, like webtoons or comics that are coming out during the week. Even any extracurricular activities that I have coming up go into my agenda, which helps me stay organized. I have also started using Google Calendar on my phone, where I colour code everything to keep me on track. This helps me not forget my homework and other responsibilities I have.

Another thing I have learned is that even if I have to work a lot harder than other students, it's also important to keep everything in balance. Staying happy and motivated is more important than anything else. So if I'm late for a homework assignment, I've learned not to stress over it as much as I used to earlier. It's a challenge sometimes and I still have to work on that, but I'm learning to set realistic expectations for myself. Part of the process is talking to your teachers and letting them know if you need more time to complete your work. Most teachers will be very supportive if you show them that you actually want to do well. For example, I have asked my teachers in the past if I can retake a test and so far every one of them has said yes to it. Some teachers have also noticed that I do much better if I am allowed to answer questions out loud versus if I have to write them down. So I have been lucky enough to be quizzed verbally.

I still have to work hard to get good grades and when I write stories for my blog, it takes three or four drafts but it's worth the trouble. I love writing. I love it because I can express myself and write about my feelings and interests; I find it easier to write about my thoughts than talking about them. I'm very proud to say that it is due to these changes that school is no longer a place I feel anxious about. Of course, I still have my bad days. But I've learned to focus on the positive, even if it is small, simple positives. Some challenges remain, like getting anxious about tests, but things have gotten better. I've learned to do my best to learn around my learning disabilities. I try out different things all the time. While I am still disappointed sometimes when a test might not have gone as well as I had thought, I always push myself to do better the next time and to believe in myself.

I feel the most important thing is to accept yourself for who you are and to never give up on yourself. Don't let anyone put you down and always remember to believe in yourself. There is a saying by Leonard Cohen: 'There is a crack in everything. That's how the light gets in.' I see that now. No one is perfect; even if it may seem to you like there is a perfect girl or boy in your class, remember there is no such thing as perfection. Everyone has cracks, but that is what makes us unique and special in the best way possible.

I write about my learning disability because I want to let the world know that having a disability isn't a bad thing. The way I see it now is that I have a little friend living in my brain and its name is learning disability. Just like with my real friends, there are good days and bad days with this friend too. But learning disability has taught me many good things too, such as not giving up and the importance of hard work. It has made me more empathetic and stronger. I know now that it is okay to be different and to learn differently. When I was nine, I couldn't even write a complete paragraph. Who would have thought that two years later I would be writing this chapter! Be kind to yourself, especially when you are having a rough time. It got better for me and I know it will get better for you too. Treat yourself to a day off on weekends instead of studying and just have fun. If things get tough, never forget who you are and that you are strong. There is only one of you in this world and you are important. Your strength might be hiding under your anxiety and insecurities, but it's there. You just need to find it.

5

Ravdanur Cuma

SYRIA AND TURKEY

GROWING up, I never thought that one day my country would face a war and that we would have to immigrate to another country.

I was raised in Idlib, a small city in northwestern Syria that borders Turkey. It's a very green city with lots of trees and flowers. There are nine children in my family and I'm in the middle of four older siblings and four younger siblings. All my older siblings are already married, so I've been the oldest in the house for a long time.

I was still very young when my family had to leave Syria because of the conflict there. When the war started, I did not even realize it was a war. I kept asking my father, 'Why is this happening?' and he always told me to not be afraid, that everything will be fine and that we would have peace. Since then my memories of our home are often overshadowed by the conflict and our fight for survival. But I do remember how normal my life was before that. I went to school, played with my friends and spent time with my family. I was happy. The garden in my school is one of the things I remember most vividly. It was beautiful. We had this courtyard that was full of old trees. My classmates and I would carve our names into those trees. I hope to be able to go back one day and see if my name is still there.

The crisis in Syria started in 2011 and that was the end of my childhood as I knew it. All sense of normalcy was gone. You grow up fast when every day is a fight to stay alive. My last eight months in Syria were spent almost entirely indoors. Our town was being bombed every day and so we had to hide for safety. I was always praying for peace, dreaming about peace. I could see that it was so needed. In my dreams, every human being was treated with dignity and respect, but when I opened my eyes, I could see children were dying and women were suffering. The situation got so bad that my family spent the last three months there underground. Along with our friends and neighbours, we hid. It was really hard for us, always dark and cold. My siblings and I were always asking our mother what was going on. We wanted to go home, we wanted to sleep in our own rooms, we were so tired. There wasn't enough food, so we were always hungry. Everyone had to split everything, which meant we all had only a little bit to eat.

One day, my father told us it was no longer safe for us to stay there and we had to leave Syria at once. A lot of us from the city decided to flee together. I asked my dad to go back to our house to get my clothes and things from my room. He told me we didn't have enough time to do that, but that we'd be back in a month or two as soon as the government addressed the conflict and came up with a solution. We had no idea that we wouldn't be able to return for years … we still don't know if we will ever be able to return.

We fled in the night. The journey to Turkey took about five hours on foot. When we arrived at the Turkish border, the army was waiting there for us with food and blankets because it was so cold. They took us to a refugee centre where they registered our names, took our pictures and fingerprints, and gave us IDs.

Our life as refugees started in a tent camp close to the border. It was truly hard for us there, especially in the beginning. I would be very afraid during the nights. I was always crying to my father that I wanted to go home and I didn't want to be in that strange place anymore. I would ask him so many questions. Why are we here? Did our house get bombed? Do we still have a home? He would reassure me that we would be able to go back, that we just had to be patient. He told me that we had come to Turkey because it's safe and we could all be together. If we had stayed at home, we would have died.

The fear was all consuming for my siblings and I. My dad decided that we all needed to learn Turkish, not only because we'd need it in this new country but also to keep our minds off of the bad things happening and how afraid we all were. He enrolled us in a Turkish course in the refugee camp. I was surprised to find out that I was really good at Turkish. I became almost fluent in two months. I really enjoyed learning a new language and focusing on something other than our situation.

After a while, we moved to a container camp in Kilis and started our life afresh. It was better than the tent camp. I was able to go to school again. We never forgot what had happened or what we had been through, but for the first time we were able to be busy with other things and be children again. We were able to focus on the future, and look beyond just survival.

I was able to finish my secondary school in Kilis. But during my time there I realized I was in minority. Child marriage was forcing my friends and peers to drop out from school at an alarming rate. It's hard to blame parents for this. Families were strapped for income. None of us knew what would happen tomorrow and parents worried what would happen to their daughters if they died. In such precarious situations, families felt that marrying their daughters off often seemed like the best way to secure their and the family's future.

My best friend was one of the many girls who got married in our camp. I cried the day it happened because I knew that she would not be able to come to school anymore and I would not be able to see her. I had tried to speak with her father, but he had kicked me out of the house. He told me I wasn't allowed to speak with his daughter anymore because I was a bad example for her, and that she had said she didn't want to get married because of me.

As I watched girls around me drop out and get married, I knew that I wasn't ready for that. I wanted to be a student, not a wife or a mother. I didn't want to have a child when I was still one myself. At the age of fourteen, how could I be ready to take on the responsibility of becoming a parent? I was scared of the idea of being forced to live with a strange man. I wanted to live at home. I wanted to see my teachers and read my books. I want to start a family one day, but I wasn't ready for it then.

People came to see my father to try to arrange a match for me. But he stood by me and refused them. If it weren't for his support, I'd be married and would have had many children by now. I imagine my life would have been very hard then because I wouldn't have had the ability to provide for my children and feed them. But because my father believed in me and supported me, I was able to continue my education. It wasn't easy. Every day was a battle. I felt like I was in the midst of two wars: the war in Syria and the war in the camp to try to go to school. But I kept at it. I tried to be a role model for other girls in my community by speaking out against child marriage and showing other girls that I was continuing my education. I wanted to show my peers that there was a different path possible, besides marriage.

I started to speak up before journalists and people in the camp. I spoke to other families and tried to tell them to send their daughters to school. Oftentimes I was met with resistance. Parents saw me as a bad example. But I continued my advocacy and finished high school. I even got a scholarship to study political science and international relations at university.

I left the camp to start university, but I didn't stop my advocacy. Turkey is hosting more than 3.5 million Syrian refugees and there is a need to remind my community about the importance of education for women. I started to speak at conferences and TV programmes. I met with refugees on the ground and tried to raise awareness about the importance of educating refugee girls.

While I was studying and doing my advocacy, I also started working to support my family. I first worked as a translator (my father was right, learning Turkish really did pay off), and later I taught other students Arabic. With the money I earned, I was able to help my parents and siblings leave the refugee camp and live elsewhere. My education saved my family and helped us start a new life. My father likes to say now that he gave me the freedom to study and because of that I had the ability to save our family. He tells other parents to think about what their daughters are capable of doing. He shows them how much better their lives and the lives of everyone in our community would be if every girl could go to school, earn a salary and achieve her ambitions. Together we're trying to convince families to let their daughters learn.

In 2016, I decided to formalize my advocacy work into a nonprofit organization. I named it Ravdanur, after myself. I wanted to name it after myself because I wanted Syrians everywhere to see my name, learn from my example, and know that they could follow the same. Ravdanur came from the same set of pressures and difficult situations. If she was able to succeed, then maybe others can too.

Ravdanur works to improve living standards of refugees in Turkey, focusing on girls' and boys' education, health and protection. We advocate against child marriage and implement projects to try to prevent it. To date, my organization has supported thousands of children, helping them return to school and providing them with the materials they need to learn.

My work has received some fantastic recognition. In 2015, the president of Turkey heard about my efforts and invited me to a special ceremony where I received joint Turkish citizenship. He told me that he was proud of me not only as a Syrian citizen, but also as a Turkish citizen. Since then, I've spoken at places like the United Nations in New York and at the European Parliament to advocate for refugee rights.

Due to my success, a lot of people in my community look at me differently now. Girls are asking me how they can get a university scholarship or live in a dorm or learn Turkish. I always help them and make sure they know about all the opportunities available to students. I'm so proud that they see my example and understand that they too can do everything I've done. With Ravdanur, I had the opportunity to go back to the camp my family and I used to live in, but this time as part of the humanitarian relief efforts. I was able to help the people who at one point told me I was a bad example. I was really proud that I was able to support their children. People would ask me if I was the same Ravdanur that used to be in that camp. They wanted to take pictures with me or invite me to their containers for coffee or a visit. I spoke at my former school and told girls about applying to universities and the opportunities available to them—and also about the disadvantages of getting married early.

I have also gotten many opportunities to visit my homeland Syria while working with the International Blue Crescent Foundation (IBC) from Turkey. We often meet with other

Syrians who are still suffering because of the war, now over a decade long. Sometimes we provide them shelter, sometimes food and sometimes we just give them hope by telling them that they are not alone. With IBC, we have managed to make many women and children smile. They have hope—hope that this war will end soon, that they will go back to their homes, their children to their schools and the sick to hospital—just like any other human being.

No matter where I am, my goal is always the same: ensuring that every Syrian girl is able to continue her education and choose if or when she wants to get married. I also want all Syrians to remember that we did not choose to be born as refugees and the war is not our fault, that we must be strong and know our rights, that we must fight for peace and share humanity and compassion. As I've explained, my work takes me from the homes of refugees living in container camps to the halls of the UN. Something I've noticed when I attend events—particularly events about Syrian refugees—is how very few Syrian refugees are part of these conversations. It's impossible to make any decisions about refugees' futures without including the refugees themselves. Our voices need to be a part of any solution.

Many fellow refugees risk their lives hoping for a better life somewhere else in the world, hoping for a better future, more peaceful life. I hope one day there will be no more fights, no more war, and for peace to be the aim for all of humanity. When countries and politicians say they do not want refugees coming in, I feel so bad because the war is not our fault. I had to fight for my rights, but that shouldn't be the case. Nonetheless, I accepted the challenge and fought for my rights and will fight for peace. I faced lots of challenges and difficulties in my immigration journey, but that story makes me Ravdanur Cuma.

My dream is to one day return to my country. I am using my time away to educate and improve myself so that when I return to Syria, I can return as an education minister or someone who can help lead the rebuilding effort. That is my dream.

6

Anjeli

INDIA

ILIVE on a tea plantation in Assam, India's largest tea-
producing state. I love the greenery and scenic beauty of the
tea plantations. There is so much lush greenery here and you can
always see women in the fields plucking tea leaves. I love that
beauty.

Most of my community lives and works on the tea plantations.
They work for minimum wage, which is about Rs 167 per
day. I see mothers struggle to support their families with that
wage. Many of the people who work on the plantations aren't
very educated, and yet they invest a lot of their earnings in the
education of their children.

That's the case for my family. My mother and elder sister both work on the tea plantations, and the responsibility to provide for our family rests on their shoulders. My father died when I was very young. After he passed away, my mother needed my elder sister to stay at home to look after my two brothers and I. So my sister has never been to school, but she works hard to ensure that we are able to go to school. My elder brother studied up to eighth grade before getting married and beginning work as a daily wage earner. My younger brother is currently studying in eighth grade.

Every day my elder sister tells me how important it is that I study and continue my education. She knows the value of education because she was denied it. Her words always inspire me to continue my studies. My mother is also an inspiration. It's a daily struggle for her to ensure she can support our education. Even though my sister couldn't be educated, our mother makes sure that my brothers and I are sent to school.

A lot of families don't support their children equally, the way my family does. I see a lot of inequality between girls and boys in terms of opportunities. Boys have all the opportunities. Parents think that when they grow old, their sons will be the ones who will look after them. So they think it's important to take care of their sons and give them more love and opportunities. Parents don't want to invest in their daughters because they believe that daughters will eventually go live with another family after marriage and look after her in-laws instead.

There's also a lot of suspicion around girls and their activities. This is the reason girls are given less freedom than boys. Boys are never asked questions like 'Where were you?' or 'Where did you go?', but if a girl comes home late, people ask her a lot of questions.

Due to such inequality in our community, girls are much more likely to drop out of school. There are a lot of other reasons too why this happens. One of them is that the tea plantation companies give employees housing benefits, but only to those who work for them permanently. So if your family member who works at the plantation dies, your family loses their housing unless someone else from your family takes their place. Often that responsibility to ensure the family can continue staying in the same house falls on the girl. The girl has to quit school and take up a permanent job at the plantation.

Girls are always seen as a source of income. So if there is a money issue in a family, girls have to quit school and start working to fill that financial gap. If a girl is already studying in a school, the cost of buying her books and other school supplies becomes too much of a challenge when her family is already pressed for money.

Finally, the middle and high school are not near the plantation where I live. It takes very long to reach those, which forces girls to drop out. It's even harder to get there during the rainy season, so girls miss classes, which eventually forces them to drop out. It can also be unsafe for girls to walk that far all alone. At every stage, it feels like girls are forced to drop out.

When I was younger, I didn't really understand what school was all about. I went to school to play with my friends and eat together, before returning home. My earliest memories of school aren't of lessons but of its social aspects. As I got older, I realized that school is so much more than that. My teachers taught me right from wrong and made sure I had the capabilities and capacities to achieve my dreams. They prepared me for a life outside of the tea plantations and in a career of my choosing.

After I finished middle school, I was promoted to high school. In the beginning, I made many new friends. It was amazing to have friends because the journey to high school was over 3 km each way, which is far and scary if you're by yourself. My new friends and I would walk to school together and come home together, so none of us had to be alone. But after a while, all of them got bicycles and I was left behind. I'd watch them as they rode away, while I continued to walk because my family could not afford one for me. Walking 6 km for school every day is a challenge. It was even more of a challenge during the rainy season because I didn't have an umbrella. My uniform would get soaking wet in the rain, not to mention incredibly muddy and dirty. I was also teased by my peers at school because of that. I was always scared while walking alone because men who were daily wage workers would call out to me and tease me. Often I would have to miss class because I wasn't able to get to school and my performance suffered. I was falling behind in math because I couldn't attend its class regularly.

My life changed in tenth grade when my mother bought me a bicycle with the money she had saved. She knew the challenges I was facing in getting to school. She was aware that spending so much time and energy walking every day was affecting my grades. With my bicycle, I was not only able to attend my classes but also special study sessions for my exams regularly and perform better in school. I was able to rejoin my classmates in their journey to school and make friends again.

After tenth grade I started attending Lakhimpur National Academy, which is 7 km away from my home. As the school is so far, I can't ride my cycle anymore but instead need to take an auto. The auto fare costs Rs 60 every day. My mother gives me Rs 700 each month for my commute, which isn't enough. So, every month I have to miss classes when I don't have enough money. The issue is that my mother thinks the commute costs are about Rs 30 a day and I don't want to correct her. She already has a lot of burden and works so hard to give me the Rs 700 each month. I don't want to ask her for more than that. I do feel terrible when I have to skip school, being absent for even one day is a big loss for me. But I know this is the best my family can do for me right now.

Despite the challenges in getting to school, it's worth it once I get there. Lakhimpur National Academy is an amazing place. My teachers are incredible. They're so good at explaining their subjects. When students have trouble understanding a concept, our teachers don't move on. They continue explaining until they're sure we understand it. I've also finally been able to make good friends. Whenever I have to skip class because I can't afford to get there, my friends take notes and share it with me the next day. My teachers also call me if I miss school to find out why I wasn't in class and tell me what lessons I missed. I love this relationship between students and teachers.

Before I started attending Lakhimpur National Academy, I didn't even know what grammar was. But now that I'm studying here I have started learning grammar, English grammar particularly. I have since learned some English words and it's the subject I score the highest marks in! I have also been able to compete in sports since I started attending the academy and have also stood first in a quiz competition. It was the best feeling in the world when my teacher was congratulating me on my victory.

Another thing about my life that has changed is that I have joined the Purva Bharati Educational Trust (PBET), which is a Malala Fund-supported organization that supports girls and women in my community. PBET called my brother one day and told him that they were looking for girls like me to be education promoters and talk to girls who had dropped out of school about why it's important to continue their education. My brother told me I should join them and that I would be perfect for this opportunity.

I attended a meeting for PBET education promoters and learned more about what I could do to support girls' education in my tea plantation. I knew I wanted to join them and help other girls learn. As an education promoter, I worked on a project where we did a survey to find out how many girls were going to school in my community and how many had dropped out. I spoke to the girls who had dropped out to find out their reasons and explained how they can re-enrol in school. I spoke to girls who did go to school and asked if they're attending class regularly. PBET used the information from my survey to ensure they're addressing the barriers to education that affect girls the most.

Another part of my work with PBET is painting wall murals with messages about the importance of girls' education. The art raises awareness among girls and their parents about why going to school is so crucial and starts important conversations. I also meet girls and their parents together to encourage them to send their daughters to school. I tell them how education empowers girls and gives them a sense of what is right and what is wrong. It allows girls to not only pursue their parents' dreams, but their own dreams as well and also bring development and progress to the plantation. As an education promoter I receive a small stipend, which I'm using to pay for my commute so that I can attend school regularly.

I'm doing as much as I can to ensure that other girls in my community can also go to school, but the government needs to intervene as well. The government should build secondary schools and higher secondary schools within the plantations also, so that students—especially girls—can continue their studies. There would be so many more girls attending school if they didn't have to deal with commute expenses and so many other challenges just to get to school. Girls would then be able to attend school regularly, even during the rainy season. Even if they don't have any friends to go with, they wouldn't be afraid of going to school alone if it was nearby.

Earlier, I dreamt of getting a government job when I grew up so that I could provide for my family and secure our future. Perhaps in the railway department. But ever since I have become an education promoter, my mother has been observing me help other girls continue their education. She now tells me that I should become a teacher instead. She says that if I get a job in the railway department, it will of course secure our family's future. But if I become a teacher, I can help many more girls get an education and secure their own family's future. My mother believes that as a teacher I'll be able to bring a large-scale change in my community. She says that one day my name will be known not only in our community in Assam, but all across India.

7

Husnah Kukundakwe

UGANDA

I BEGAN swimming when I was three years old. Before I started swimming, I was always very shy. I don't have a lower right hand and only have three fingers on my left hand, so whenever I was around people, I would to try to hide my disability. Once I began swimming, I started to become more confident. I just loved the feeling of being in water and how free I felt in it. As time went on, I came to realize that I also really enjoyed the sport of swimming itself. I liked the challenge and the competition. I also liked how good I was at it. I was fast and powerful in water.

I'll never forget my first swimming competition. I was six years old at the time. I remember looking forward to it and feeling so excited to compete. I swam in my first race and did well. I was getting ready for my second race when I found out the teacher had swapped me for another girl, an able-bodied girl. At first, I was just so disappointed to not be able to swim. Then I got angry that my teacher had replaced me because of my disability. I couldn't believe she was underestimating me like that. The unfortunate reality is that people in Uganda aren't always kind to people with disabilities like mine. They don't see us as normal and don't think we can do what able-bodied people can do.

Even now it makes me furious to think of the six-year-old me denied the chance to compete because I have a disability. But in the long run, I proved that teacher, and everyone else who doubted me, wrong. Today I'm one of Uganda's only active para-swimmers, representing my country at international competitions around the world—and I'm much faster now than that girl my teacher had replaced me with.

After that first initial meet, I kept swimming in local races. In 2018, when I was ten years old, I discovered para-swimming. I hadn't known about its existence until then because I hadn't seen any other swimmers with disabilities in Uganda; everyone I competed against was able-bodied. When I found out about para-swimming and discovered this community of other swimmers with disabilities, I knew I wanted to be part of it. They made me want to inspire other people the way they had inspired me.

I learned that to be able to participate in para-swimming competitions, you need to get your classification. Classification is like a swimming test where Paralympic officials observe how you swim, assess your disability, and then assign you a class so that you compete against other athletes with similar impairments. In 2018, I got my first classification. At present, I'm in S9, SB8 and SM9 class. 'S' represents freestyle, backstroke and butterfly strokes, 'SB' means breaststroke and 'SM' means individual medley. In these classes, I compete against other people who also have similar disabilities. But since I'm so young and haven't finished growing yet, I'll have another classification review when I'm sixteen to confirm what class I'm in.

When I travelled to Nairobi for my initial classification and thereafter competed in the championships, I was able to race against fellow para-swimmers for the first time in my life.

Back home in Uganda, it can be dejecting to race only against able-bodied people. Seeing so many other para-swimmers and people with disabilities similar to mine made me feel so comfortable. Discovering that there was this whole world of para-swimming created for athletes like me changed my life. I only wished I had known about it sooner. I know I would have worked harder and been more motivated. But I didn't dwell on the past and focused on moving forward. I knew I had to really dedicate myself to my training if I wanted to qualify for more international para-swimming competitions. So that's what I did.

After the competition in Nairobi, I qualified to represent my country at competitions like the Tokyo 2020 Paralympics, the Singapore World Para Swimming World Series 2019 and the London 2019 World Para Swimming Allianz Championships. I get nervous before my races because I'm the only para-swimmer from Uganda, so the pressure to make my country proud rests solely on my shoulders. But I practice deep breathing and visualize the race, which usually helps get over my nerves and get geared up.

A lot has changed in my life since I got my classification and started competing at international para-swimming competitions.

Through swimming, I've been able to travel around the world for races, meet different people, and discover new things that I would have never seen otherwise. In South Korea, I swam in an indoor pool for the first time, which was both exciting and freezing—something I had never expected since I am used to swimming in cold, outdoor pools. When I went to the UK, I took a ride on the London Eye. In Singapore, I swam in an infinity pool; I thought I would get in and fall off the balcony—but that didn't stop me from trying.

But the biggest change in my life is the way I see myself now. Before I started swimming, I was really shy. I would always put on long-sleeved shirts to hide my arm and put my hand in my pocket to try to hide my fingers. But as a swimmer, you're constantly taking your clothes off, having your body on display as you jump into the pool. I had to get used to that and when I did, I saw my self-esteem rise.

The confidence I achieved in the pool helped me feel more comfortable in the classroom. My first days of primary school weren't easy. Kids would stare at me or laugh at me or try to touch my hand, which was extremely annoying. One of my teachers, Teacher Hope, saw what was happening and helped me understand that I shouldn't hide myself or my hand. She would make me the class captain or give me responsibilities like distributing everyone's books so that I don't feel different from the other kids. After I came back from my swimming classification, I felt more confident in myself. It was then that I decided to run for school prefect. I wanted to see if my peers accepted me for who I was by voting for me. They did. Becoming the school prefect and realizing that my friends and classmates believed in me was an amazing moment.

A lot of people know who I am now because of my success as a para-swimmer. When I realized that my story could motivate people, I decided to use my platform to increase awareness about the issues I care about: breaking down stereotypes of people with disabilities and helping girls go to school.

As I've said earlier, it's not easy to be a person with disabilities in Uganda. Overall, my country is an amazing place. The weather is great. You can go to parks and see wildlife like gorillas, elephants and crocodiles. There are so many kind people. But the issue is Ugandans aren't kind to people with disabilities. Parents here often abandon their children if they are born with a disability. Children with disabilities do not receive the support they need to pursue their dreams. Since they don't have a lot of opportunities, they often end up begging for money, food and clothes.

Through my story and accomplishments in the pool, I hope to pave the way for other young people with disabilities. I want to be the one to show them that contrary to what most Ugandans say, they are normal and they are capable of achieving whatever they set their minds to. I want to encourage them to come out of hiding and to aim for things they've always dreamt of doing. I want to show parents that with their support their children with disabilities can accomplish amazing things. I want to encourage parents to provide their children with the resources they need to thrive, so that they have access to the same opportunities as children without disabilities.

I also want to raise awareness about para-sports in Uganda. Three years ago, I didn't know para-swimming existed. Now I'm training to qualify for the Paralympics. I can only imagine how many other potential para-athletes are out there who just don't know para-sports exist. In addition to raising awareness, I also hope to encourage the government and leaders to invest in para-sports. Since there are no other para-swimmers in Uganda, due to lack of awareness and funding, I have to train with and compete against non-disabled athletes at home. I am lucky because my parents work very hard to cover my training fees to swim in the pool, my coach's salary, the commute costs to get to the pool and my plane tickets for international competitions. We are not rich. It is a challenge to pay for all of those expenses when my parents also have to cover the school tuition fees for my siblings and I. Across the continent of Africa, because governments dedicate very little funds to para-sports, many para-athletes from low- and middle-income countries can't afford to compete. You can see the results of this at international events: at the 2016 Rio Paralympics, only 10 of the 593 para-swimmers were from Africa. I hope to bring a change in my country, so that I am no longer the only Ugandan para-swimmer when I go to these events.

Finally, I want to use my platform from swimming to raise awareness about girls' education in Uganda. Many girls in villages or rural areas have to stop their education in primary school itself because of teenage pregnancy or forced marriage or because they don't have enough money to continue their studies. It makes me so sad knowing they could be the leaders of tomorrow but aren't able to realize their full potential. By ending their education that early, girls don't have the chance to figure out what they actually want to become or see how far they can go.

I've been trying to spread the message in my community by explaining to girls why they need to continue with their education and also encouraging their parents to support them. My mom has been helping me out with it. Together we post about the importance of girls' education on my social media. We're also thinking of starting a foundation so that I have an avenue to create change. Through the foundation, I hope to go to different schools and talk to kids about disabilities and girls' education and to raise awareness about these issues and break stereotypes. My parents could talk to other parents about their experiences and encourage them to not abandon their kids just because they have disabilities, but to love them for who they are.

Being a girl and, moreover, being a girl with a disability comes with a lot of challenges. I have been teased, called names, discriminated against, underestimated and more. But I've refused to let other people's expectations of me shape my expectations for myself. Through my leadership and accomplishments inside and outside the pool, I hope to show other girls and young people with disabilities that they should believe in themselves, and not let other people determine their path. They should follow their own dreams and passions.

8

Shereen Kanwal

PAKISTAN

MY home city of Karachi is a place that is very close to my heart. It's a coastal city known for its beaches, economic and industrial activity and amazing food. Karachi is full of people of different backgrounds and ethnicities, speaking different languages, but everyone living in harmony. It is known as the city of hearts because everyone is welcome there and I love it because of that.

I grew up in a neighbourhood in Karachi. My school was just a short walk away from my home, where I studied from first grade to the tenth. Despite living in such a densely populated area, one of the things I remember most about my school was how open and spacious it was. If I close my eyes, even now I can visualize everything about the building and classrooms.

In a class of thirty students, I was the one who sat right in front because I loved to talk. I was famous for that in school. Adults would always tell me that I should become a lawyer because I had such a way with words and spoke so beautifully. Even though it has been several years since I graduated, my teachers still remember me as a chatterbox.

While I enjoyed learning, I didn't always love school. I remember sitting at my desk, watching the clock, waiting for recess to begin or class to end. I used to think that teachers were cruel people who didn't do much. We children were the ones who had to do homework, get to school early and do all the work; what did teachers really do?

It was my ninth grade biology teacher, Yasir, who changed not only my opinion of teachers but also made me want to become one. At the beginning of the term, Yasir asked us students what we thought of teachers and the profession of teaching. Being outspoken as I am, I told him my views. He promised that by the end of the term, he would change my opinion.

Through Yasir's dedication to his students and passion for moulding our minds, I realized how influential a teacher can be. He helped me see how teachers make every other career possible. I remember once he drew a diagram on the board of a small planter out of which branches were sprouting. Each branch was a different profession—engineering, medicine, law, etc. It was then that I realized that at the root of all of those different branches/ occupations were teachers. Teachers guide the unstructured thoughts children have about their careers and help them realize their ambitions. So I decided to become one.

I graduated from school in tenth grade and enrolled in my two-year college course to prepare to go to university where I planned on studying to become a teacher. I had just taken my exams at the end of the year when I received a marriage proposal. Usually, the eldest sibling gets married off first, followed by the younger siblings. I have a sister who is six years older to me, but my parents decided to accept the proposal for me. At the age of eighteen, my parents married me off and I became a wife.

After I got married, I received the results of my college exams and found that I had failed in math. In Pakistan, if you fail in a subject, you can retake its exam to clear it. I attempted the math exam twice after that, but since I had a lot of domestic responsibilities as a new wife and daughter-in-law, I couldn't devote the time and energy needed to prepare and failed each time.

Yet I was not deterred from my goal. I was preparing to take the math exam for the third time when my in-laws began to discourage me from taking it. They told me it was no use to attempt it again when I had already failed twice, and that it didn't matter anyway since they didn't want me to have a professional career. This was quite shocking for me. Before I was married off, my in-laws were supportive of my education; they had even promised my parents and I that I would be allowed to pursue my higher education and a professional career. But things changed after marriage and they did not uphold their promises. At that point in my life, there were only two things I hated the most: math and my in-laws.

In addition to these challenges, I was also facing some behavioural issues with my husband. He was just two years older than me—such a young age to be married. He was not financially stable and inconsistent with his occupation, which contributed to a lot of financial issues. My husband could not provide for my needs. My parents tried to intervene and speak with my in-laws and husband, but things were only going downhill.

I got pregnant about a year after we got married. When I was four months pregnant, there was an incident of domestic violence when my husband beat me. When I lost the baby soon after that, I decided I could no longer live with him. I had compromised on a lot of things: the lack of support for my education and career, my in-laws' behaviour, our lack of financial stability—but domestic violence was one thing I could not tolerate. A man who does not care for my safety is not someone I can live with or be with for the rest of my life. So, a year and a half after we were married, I divorced my husband.

I thought it would be somewhat easy to transition back to my parents' home after the divorce. I had lived there my whole life and I had only been gone for a little over a year. But I was wrong. My extended family had completely changed their attitude towards me. In Pakistan, your extended family has a lot of influence on your life. The same people who used to tell me that I spoke so beautifully and was so pretty were now telling me to talk less, stop laughing out loud and stop wearing loud clothes and make-up. Once when I was planning to attend the wedding of my cousin, certain superstitious family members told me to not go near the bride because I was divorced. Those remarks wounded me to the core.

It was a very difficult time for me. I had suffered so much— and now I was suffering at the hands of my family and community for ending a bad marriage. I started to feel like I no longer had an identity or purpose in life. I had asked if I could resume my education after the divorce, but my family discouraged me, particularly my mother's side. What would people say about a divorced woman studying outside the house and having a professional career? What would my former in-laws think about me doing this? I was trapped within the four walls of the house.

It was so frustrating when I thought about how our society treats an unmarried forty-year-old woman. She is allowed to have her professional career, she can wear loud make-up and clothes, she's allowed to live her own life. But if you're like me, divorced at the age of nineteen, there are completely different expectations from you. I wasn't allowed to live my life anymore. My family was pressurizing me to get married again, telling me that was the only solution to my predicament. It seemed as though I was only allowed to have my own identity and life once I had an identity through a spouse. I couldn't restart my life on my own.

One day, I was complaining to God about how unfair everything that had happened to me was—and at such a young age. Then I realized that I shouldn't be focused on the past, but instead think about the future and how my new situation is allowing me opportunities that were denied to me earlier. God had given me this opportunity to finally pursue what I love and achieve the things I had aspired for when I was younger. That's when I resurrected all the dreams that I had buried when I had got married. I spoke to my parents about continuing my education. Even though there was still resistance from my extended family, my mother was my champion.

My younger sister was preparing for college at the time, although she was not as good a student as me. My mother decided that my sister should apply to a college in the nearby city of Hyderabad, where college admissions are easier; and used that as a cover to also allow me to enrol. I would study at home, in Karachi, but go to Hyderabad occasionally with my sister for the exams. I taught at a local school to earn money for my tuition. Of course, family members were upset about this decision. They said I should not be allowed to interact with male coworkers or male students. But despite this resistance and negativity, I continued with it and earned enough money to pay for my own education in secret.

I studied in secret for over a year before my father found out. Then my mother helped convince my father and our family to be supportive of my education and professional career, as opposed to having me married me off as soon as possible again.

I am an avid follower of the news. I'm always watching it. One day while I was studying in college in Hyderabad, I was watching a morning show and I saw Selma Alma, the founder of Durbeen. She was announcing a government institute with a bachelor's programme that also provided financial support for underprivileged students. I realized this was fate intervening and that this could be the perfect opportunity for me. I applied, was accepted and am now attending GECE Hussainabad, where I'm currently studying to complete my degree so that I can become a teacher in a public school. My journey till here hasn't always been easy and there were many occasions when I was not sure if this would actually happen, but through it all I never gave up on my ambitions.

In my current job as a private school teacher and possibly as a public school teacher in future, I hope I can be a confidante to my students. I want them to feel like they can express themselves safely before me. I want to be an outlet and a resource for my girl students, who might not have anyone else to discuss with what's on their mind, the challenges they're facing or the problems they're having such as the pressure to drop out of school. As someone who has faced barriers to her education and challenges from her own family, I know what they could be going through and can help them have conversations with their families.

If you were to strike a conversation with me, you would realize I'm a very convincing person. I used to think I would use my power with words to become a lawyer, but now I see that my skills will be best used to help convince girls, their families and communities to allow the girls to continue their education. As a teacher, an activist and a motivational speaker, I now tell my story to help other girls and women see that they have the confidence and strength to pursue their dreams just as I did.

9

Mungli Hasda

INDIA

WHEN I was young, my favourite subject in school was Assamese. I liked learning how to read and write stories in the language of my home state of Bodoland Territorial Region (BTR) Assam in Northeast India. I've been studying for many years now—I am currently in my fifth semester at the university. But throughout my education, my favourite subject has remained the same.

Now that I live far away from my family, studying Assamese reminds me of where I am from. It is my own subject, a language I've known since I was very young and is easy for me to understand. Though I have had a hard time with some other subjects in school, Assamese has always come naturally to me. I even hope to one day earn a master's degree in it.

Although BTR Assam is my home, my life there has not always been easy there. I was born in a relief camp near the forest village of Nazirapur, where displaced people from my community seek shelter after losing their homes. In BTR Assam, many families like mine have had to leave their villages due to violent conflicts between armed insurgent groups or environmental degradation such as floods and droughts. The houses in Nazirapur are not of good quality. They are made of materials like plastic and clay, and are not built to withstand such calamities.

After living for seven months in a relief camp, my family was able to rebuild our house and return to Nazirapur. I was a baby then, so my earliest memories are of my childhood in my village. I have many happy memories from this period, especially of times when I played games with other children in my neighborhood. But my family and I faced many difficulties. There was no good public school near my village, so I had no choice but to enrol in a private school for my primary education. My family has always been supportive of my learning, but the cost of sending me to a private school put a strain on our finances. It was also very difficult to commute to school because there was no public transportation available. I walked several kilometres to school every day with my friends from the village. At times, I would have to make the trip alone. This made me fear for my safety, especially on my way home in the evenings with armed forces patrolling the area.

During this time, I often stressed about whether or not I would be able to complete my education. I have seen poverty since childhood, so I've always known how important it is to study and how education determines one's future. But if my family could not pay the school fees, I knew I would have to drop out soon. So I decided to find work to help my family pay for my education. I found a job as a domestic worker in someone's house and lived there while I went to school. Working there was difficult sometimes, but I was determined to keep up with my studies so that I would be able to stand on my own feet one day. With my wages, I was able to pay my school fees and even put enough money together to help my parents with their household expenses. I missed my family, but I knew it was not possible for them to support me in their situation.

One day, my two friends and I were brought to the train station in Kokrajhar by men who said they had a work opportunity for us. We did not understand what was happening at the time— but we were about to be trafficked to Gujarat, an Indian state on the opposite coast from Assam.

But before my friends and I could be put on the train to Gujarat, representatives from the Malala Fund-supported organization Nedan Foundation intervened. They took us to Destination Girls Home (DGH), a shelter home for trafficking survivors, rescued domestic workers and out-of-school girls in Kokrajhar. I was scared at first because I had never heard about Nedan Foundation and did not know how their members had found us. I had no idea where they were taking me or how long I would be held there once I arrived. But after sleeping in the home for two to three days, I started to feel better.

The day I arrived at DGH was the turning point in my life. I met other girls like me, girls of all ages who had experienced the same hardships as I had, and we have lived together in the shelter since. With the help of Nedan Foundation, I was able to enrol in a government secondary school to finish my tenth grade. After passing my matriculation exam, I enrolled in a BA programme course at Aronai College in Kokrajhar and that's where I am right now.

Looking back, I feel grateful for everything I have learned with the help of Nedan Foundation. As a Kokrajhar-based non-profit, Nedan Foundation helps girls in Assam fight for our education and trains us to become leaders and advocates for our communities. They have clubs across my state that offer activism workshops, life skills training and classes in many different subjects to help students succeed in school. At DGH, I have access to much better facilities for studying than I ever had before, such as group study halls and desks to do homework on. We are even allowed to travel outside of Kokrajhar on group trips to other villages in India, which has helped me expand my vision of life and what I could achieve. I do not have to work in order to pay for school, which means I have time for other activities like working in our communal garden and spending time with my friends. On most days, I also help the younger girls wash their clothes and complete their homework.

My favourite part of life at DGH is all the games and sports I get to play with my friends. Since childhood, I have loved competing in athletic events—especially track and field, high jump and long jump. In 2021, I even won a trophy in my college for being the best sports player in school. I am so proud of this accomplishment that would have not have been possible before.

Although I am happy to be here today, I miss my family and the forest village I left behind to live here. This feeling is shared among many of the girls at DGH—no child wants to be away from their parents. It would be much better if girls did not have to leave their homes to receive an education and be safe from danger, trafficking and displacement.

This is why I want the Indian government to make sure that education is completely free of cost for students throughout the secondary level. This would keep the families living in poverty from having to make the difficult choice between sending their daughters to work or withdrawing them from school altogether. Our leaders should not only eliminate school fees, but also give students books—which are too expensive for many families to afford—and hostel facilities for students who are displaced and in need of shelter. Every village in India should also have schools and colleges nearby so that girls can live with their families while receiving their education and not have to walk long distances in the morning and evening. With these provisions, our lives can become much better.

Our leaders must also make sure that girls in India are able to continue their education in times of crisis. There are many girls like me who live in forest villages and don't have mobile phones or internet connection or even electricity. They have been unable to learn during the Covid-19 pandemic, and I fear many of them will not return to school when it passes. Though I am living at DGH and have support from Nedan Foundation, it has been difficult to study during the pandemic. I can't understand what's happening in my online classes properly because either my internet connection is bad or the teacher's connection is poor. When teachers hold class in-person, we are able to understand concepts, cultivate our ideas and take notes to prepare for exams. But now we are approaching the exam season and I have no notes at all. How am I supposed to pass? It is the right of all children to receive an uninterrupted education and the responsibility of our government to provide resources to facilitate that—even through a pandemic.

But even when our leaders fail us, Nedan Foundation has helped me understand that individuals and advocates can make a big difference in people's lives. If they had not found me that day at Kokrajhar Station, I might never have been able to continue my studies or receive the shelter and safety I now have at DGH. They have helped me overcome the hardships in my life so that one day I might be able to stand on my own feet. After I graduate from college, I hope I too will be able to help girls out of poverty and bring good to BTR Assam. I will start by building a school in my forest village for girls who cannot afford to study and a facility to provide shelter for them if their family loses their home. My students will learn many subjects like math, science, English and Assamese, but we will always make time for fun activities too. We will dance and play games; we will have sports competitions and give out trophies to the winners. I believe that happiness is the best remedy for hardship, and I will one day bring it back to the girls of BTR Assam.

10

Katiuska Sanchez

VENEZUELA

I WAS born in a South American country called Venezuela. It's best known for being a small Caribbean paradise with a diversity of climates. I had a normal life as a teenager—but in 2017, everything changed.

Before I go forward, I must explain a bit about the history of my country. Venezuela has been led by the same political parties since I was born in 1999. So I have never experienced a different reality than the one that exists to date in my country. Growing up, I spent my days focusing on my studies and spending time with my friends. We used to go out and do things we enjoyed, like going to the movies or eating together. It sounds like a normal life for a teenager, but in reality, Venezuela was already experiencing challenges. We lacked basic supplies, necessities were scarce and inflation was perpetually increasing. Hospitals lacked supplies to care for patients. The economic and humanitarian crises worsened with each passing day. Little by little, the enraged Venezuelans took to the streets, trying to put an end once and for all to the injustice we were experiencing as citizens, demanding employee rights and speaking out against the insecurity on the streets.

At that age, I was not able to understand much of what was happening. My mother said that someday everything would return to normal … that everything would improve. But as the situation got worse in 2014, she forbade me from attending high school out of fear that something bad would happen to me on the streets. I remember feeling worried when I found out I would not be able to study for a while. I was afraid the situation would be drawn out and that, if it did last, I might not be able to go to university, which had always been my dream.

By then, the streets were literally on fire. It was not safe to go out and much lesser for me at my young age to be alone on the streets. On days when I left the house, I was accompanied by my mother to get food and other basic necessities. Upon leaving, I only saw disaster. Police and military violated the rights of the protesters—they killed not hundreds, but thousands of innocents who were fighting for a better place to live in and pass onto their children. Many of them were young, between the ages of eighteen and twenty-six.

Those were difficult days. I kept myself occupied with reading as much as I could. One of the books that marked that moment in my life and, I can confidently say, the rest of it too, was *The Diary of Anne Frank*. That book inspired me to believe that everything I felt was okay, that being scared was okay, that not knowing how to deal with the stress was okay, that feeling anxiety wasn't wrong and that, in fact, I could find ways to deal with my anxiety and make it my friend. It was then that I decided to start writing a diary. It was not elaborate work. On the contrary, it was just the passing of my days, my daily life. Little by little, my feelings began to intensify and I realized the art of writing served as an escape and refuge to my mind. Just by writing, my mind began to create non-stop. I no longer felt fear, I just wanted to write for hours in my diary. Anne Frank had saved my life. She had become my hero.

At home, everything seemed to be quiet. My mother and I spent the days watching the news and doing our chores. She still had to go to work, so some days of the week I was alone at home. Little by little, the chaos came to an end—or so we believed. Everything seemed to return to normal. But then the situation repeated itself. Inflation ran rampant in our country. We were a nation rich in oil, but lacking in basic needs. We had one of the highest crime rates in Latin America. The life we knew began to change in a more noticeable way. Being on the streets after sundown was synonymous with danger, so much so that it became a norm to not step out at night at all. It became common knowledge that if you left the house in expensive clothing, you'd be delivering your belongings to thieves on a silver platter—whatever you went out with, you might not return with. This summarized our existence. Afraid for our lives, we allowed for this to become our new reality: more and more abuse of power, more fear among the people when they noticed that no matter how much they fought, all protests were in vain. We lost so many young people; adults and teenagers who were hungry for justice. But at the end of the day, nothing changed.

Time passed but the situation in Venezuela remained the same. The government made it seem like things were okay, but it wasn't so; it had been months of uncertainty. I had been able to return to school when things looked like they were returning to normal. In 2015, I graduated from high school and tried to realize my dream of attending university. I studied for the university exam for months, but I did not get good results. Due to my family's economic situation I couldn't afford tuition at the private universities, while the free universities lacked teachers since they couldn't pay them enough. I decided to keep learning no matter what. Since childhood, I have liked languages. I've always wanted to learn about more than just my country. I've always wanted to go out into the world and enjoy it to the fullest because learning is a gift that not everyone receives. I learnt English and dedicated myself to loving and understanding it as much as I could. The support of my mother in any extracurricular activity was motivation every day to achieve the goals that I set. My education was her priority.

In 2017, when I turned eighteen, I finished my language studies, hoping I'd be able to start my university studies once and for all; even though the reality was that my dream seemed further and further away and more unattainable. The situation was getting worse day by day, the economy was still in poor shape and my mom didn't have enough money to pay for my education. Public universities were closed for months because the teachers began to emigrate, as most of the protesters were students.

In April that year, my mother and older brother decided to send me to Panama. My brother already lived there and my mother thought it was the best option for me, even though because of the cost of the tickets, she had to stay behind in Venezuela. The week before I left, I said goodbye to my friends and family. At the time, I didn't realize what was coming and what I was leaving behind. I had no idea how much my life would change as a result of this decision. I was not aware that I had to pack eighteen years in two suitcases, which was all I could take with me. I didn't know what it would be like to adapt to a new culture, where everything would be new, where I would need to add words to my vocabulary, where I would have to make friends and connect with others because as an immigrant you are not exactly a special guest. In fact, you are the person nobody invited and many would want you to know that—sometimes in a good way, sometimes in a bad way. When I was getting ready to leave Venezuela, I cried for days, but I knew this would forge a better future for me and my family.

I learned many things in a very short span of time when I moved to Panama. I learned to take responsibility for myself, work hard, pay for food and shelter through my job as a waitress and handle the adversities that came my way. I experienced anxiety and depression. I missed my life, my home and my mother. I didn't have any friends. Everything was complicated as an immigrant, and the university there was too expensive. But I didn't have a choice—I had to be an adult one day at a time and deal with these problems. But despite how difficult it was, I am grateful for the experiences and for what I learned from each of them … for what I lived through at such a young age. In Venezuela, the situation continued to be precarious. But when I could not find opportunities to study in Panama because of the cost, I gave up the idea of living there. After eight months in Panama, I decided to return to Venezuela, hoping to find other horizons and different paths to reach my goal of attending university.

Coming back home was devastating. The memories I had of the country where I was born and grew up were no more than just that—memories. Despite having been gone for only a few months, I felt like I'd arrived in a completely different place. Many of my friends no longer lived in Venezuela, some of them were in other Latin American countries and others even further away. Thus, Venezuela began to lose its youth and its future slowly. We knew that we should leave if we had dreams and goals because it would not be possible for everyone to achieve them here. We had to leave the country for the sake of the future that we longed for.

As soon as I returned, I wanted to leave. I had the feeling that I was no longer at home, I did not feel comfortable with the quality of life, with Venezuela's new normal. I just knew that I could not remain there. Together my mother and I decided to travel to Peru. It was not an easy decision—my mother would be abandoning more than twenty-five years of work, a house that was our home for years and our family. But we went ahead. Since flights to Peru were expensive, our most viable option was to travel by land. I will always describe that trip as the most difficult experience of my life so far. During a seven-day bus trip, we travelled from my hometown of Maracay, Aragua, to Cúcuta, Colombia, from Cúcuta to Bogota, from Bogotá to Cali, from Cali to Ipiales, and from there to the Ecuadorian border. After seven days that seemed to last forever, we finally arrived in Lima.

Lima, Peru, is a magical place, rich in culture, colours, music, and people full of love. The people in Peru are warm, friendly and cordial. Despite the many cultural differences, Peru is a unique place, which opened doors and created opportunities for me that I will remember for the rest of my life. My stay there and the people I met along the way changed my view of life. They helped me see that working hard always gets rewarded, and that when you are good to others, good things happen to you. However, my goal was always the same: to be able to study. To live in Peru decently, my mom and I had to work eighteen hours per day, which left no time to study. So the moment came when, as much as I loved Peru, it was time to leave it behind. I decided to move to Chile because it is known as one of the best countries in South America. I wanted to come and see it for myself. Since arriving in Chile, I've found better opportunities to work and do things I enjoy here. I have also met people here who I can happily say are not friends, but family.

The last six years have been an incredible and difficult journey. But these experiences will help me grow and prepare me for my greatest dream: the day I'm able to study at a university. I want to study languages and be able to work as a teacher in different places around the world because through my journey I have learnt that I love travelling, meeting new people, learning new cultures, and seeing new places. So I can see my future self living in other countries, teaching young people, and doing what I enjoy the most: writing.

One day I will realize the dream I have fought so long for and study at a university. When that day comes, all of these challenges would have been worth it.

11

Rahel Sheferaw

ETHIOPIA

I WAS born in a rural community in the Amhara region of Ethiopia. It's about 130 km away from the capital city of Addis Ababa. Most of my community depends on agriculture for a living. I also come from a family of farmers. My father was one too, before he died when I was a child. Soon after the death of my father, my mother went to live in a monastery and so I grew up with my elder sister.

Like a lot of rural areas in Ethiopia, most people in my community are not educated. In the case of girls, one of the reasons is that it is often not safe for girls to travel alone. To go to the market, to collect firewood and water or to go to school, you have to pass through an uneven road where you could be taken by men. It's happened to me once too—men have tried to lure me off the path I was going on. That's why when I go to school, I go with my friends.

My school is about 3 km away from our village. There are no transportation options in my area, which means I have to walk the whole way and back. It takes me about one and a half hours each way, so I spend three hours of my day walking. I usually attend the morning shift; once I get home from school, I have lunch and then start helping my sister with the domestic work around the house. There is no time to rest. I collect firewood, fetch water, cook food for the family, wash dishes and take care of my younger brothers and sisters. It's a lot of work, but I'm happy to help my sister who takes care of all of us. After I finish all my tasks at home, I start doing my assignments for the next day at school and study for exams. It's difficult balancing both my work for school and at home, but this is common for girls in Ethiopia. Most girls lead this kind of life.

When I was in seventh grade in 2016, the elders in my community visited my sister's house several times to try to convince her to get me married. This is common when a girl turns thirteen or fourteen in my community, even though the legal minimum age for marriage in Ethiopia is eighteen. Child marriage is deep rooted in our community; so after girls complete their primary education, oftentimes their families don't allow them to continue with their secondary education. The girls I know aren't interested or willing to get married, but they usually don't have a choice. They are all frustrated. They need support from people in positions of power to support them and help them say no.

I was one of the lucky ones because I had the support of my elder sister. I discussed it with her and told her that I didn't want to marry, but instead wanted to continue my education. My sister supported my decision. She got married at the age of fifteen and knows the challenges of child marriage very well. She is already divorced from her husband and has health issues because of having children at such a young age. My sister is a role model not only for me, but also for her daughters and all the other girls who live in our village. She refused the community elders and told them that I would keep going to school.

However, the elders went to my mother in the monastery and asked for her permission to get me married. She agreed. When I heard this bad news, I reported to the school administration. The Malala Fund-supported organization Education for Sustainable Development (ESD) works in schools like mine and intervenes when girls tell them that the community elders are forcing them to get married. By talking to the religious leaders and local administration, ESD convinces elders not to force girls to get married. I knew about the work they were doing in my school, so I went to them to explain what was happening. They intervened on my behalf and told the elders that I was not old enough to get married. They explained that it was my right to decide if and when I get married and to whom. As a result, the elders cancelled my planned marriage.

ESD has a girls' club at my secondary school and as its member, I now advise other female students not to drop out of school to get married. We talk about traditional practices, child marriages, how to be successful in school and what we want to become or do in the future. I tell them about my experiences and how the organization helped me continue my education. I also educate them about the negative effects of child marriage on girls, on their parents and their community. Through the club, ESD improves girls' knowledge and skills on how to prevent and address problems like child marriage when they occur. They teach us how to negotiate with family members, elders or peers who are trying to pressurize them. Most of the girls in the club listen to my advice. I've seen them fighting to cancel their own weddings and protect themselves, just like I did.

ESD also provides girls with life skills, information about sexual health and reproductive education. In my community, there's not a lot of knowledge about sanitary napkins or even underwear and why girls should use them. During their menstruation, girls often don't go to school because they can't manage the bleeding and this eventually leads to them dropping out. That's why I teach other girls in my school how to produce and use sanitary pads. We share information, skills and knowledge during these sessions and it's also an opportunity for all of us to connect, share and discuss our ambitions. I'm proud of how I'm helping other girls stay in school and in minimizing dropouts.

Since I don't have to worry about elders forcing me to get married now, I'm able to focus on my education. My current favourite subject in school is social science, where we learn about civics, democracy and rights. I'm currently studying for my secondary school exams and hope to be able to go to university next. I hope that one day I will be able to become a lawyer. In Ethiopia, many people misinterpret laws, particularly in rural areas. There are laws in place that protect girls—like the law that says girls can't get married before the age of eighteen—but local authorities don't enforce the laws correctly. I want to be a lawyer to help save girls from child marriage by educating communities about the legal processes in place that protect girls. If the community knows the law, we can put an end to child marriages.

As part of my work when I'm older, I would also love to use technology to reach even more girls. I could create weekend programmes and clubs for girls across many different rural communities. We could connect through technology and I could tell them my story and educate them on how to avoid child marriage and help them understand that they don't have to get married. I want them to know how to respond when someone asks them to get married before they're ready or even for a sexual interaction. I want to help them develop these life skills so they can continue their education and have the tools they need to succeed at whatever it is they want to do in their future. Since I can't physically be in every community, it's through technology that I can help as many girls as possible so that they can continue with their education just like I did.

12

Anjali

INDIA

I N the mornings when I ride my bicycle to school, everyone in my village turns and stares. 'This is the girl that was out of school,' they say, 'and now she goes to school every day.' They are surprised at my success, but they are also encouraged—I am proof that it is possible for other girls to accomplish this too.

I live in a village called Alipura in the Hamirpur district of Uttar Pradesh, India. Here, everyone lives together in harmony. When you walk through Alipura, you may see girls walking to school together in small groups. This is part of a community solidarity initiative in which girls—even those who are out of school—help one another arrive safely to school on foot. This feeling of solidarity is a beautiful part of my life in Alipura.

My house is on a tree-lined street, where I live with my grandparents, parents and elder brothers. My brothers are very special to me, I feel lucky to be their younger sibling. They have completed their education and work different jobs. They're supportive of me completing my education as well and always encourage me to study despite the hardships that I sometimes experience as a girl in my community. They have told me if I ever encounter any problem, any barrier to my education, I should reach out to them and they will find me a solution.

With my brothers' support, I was able to go to school almost every day when I was younger. Though my family lives on my father's daily wages, cost was not a barrier for me because of the Right to Education Act—a constitutional mandate in India which guarantees free education for every child until the age of fourteen. My favourite part about school in those days was meeting my friends, eating lunch with them and playing together during recess. I took my elementary education for granted. I did not realize then how fortunate I was to be there at all.

But when I entered the ninth grade, my mother suddenly fell sick. With my father and brothers at work every day, I dropped out of school to take care of her. During that time, what I wanted more than anything was for my mother to get better and recover fully as soon as possible. I spent every day by her side, nursing her. But I never stopped thinking about the day I'd go back to school.

Thankfully, everyone in my household understood the dilemma I was going through. My mother, who has always supported my education, assured me that she would recover soon and encouraged me to resume my studies as soon as possible.

My father and brothers agreed as well. They decided to strike a caregiving balance so that I could re-enrol in school. They'd take turns staying home to take care of her.

So I began to consider the possibility of returning to school. But I was fourteen years old at that point and secondary education is not covered under the Right to Education Act. This means that students have to pay fees for secondary education, even if they enrol in a public school. My family had already spent a lot of money on my mother's treatment and I knew it would be difficult for us to afford my education. Even if we managed pay school fees, the cost of daily public transportation and textbooks would be too much for our income.

It was then that I met representatives from the Malala Fund-supported organization Right to Education Forum in Hamirpur district. A coalition of 10,000 educationists, non-profits, teachers' unions, networks and community members across twenty states in India, the Forum advocates for the full implementation of the Right to Education Act and the expansion of the act to ensure free education until eighteen years of age and works to increase government spending on education. As part of their work to help all girls study in Hamirpur, the Forum conducts door-to-door visits to speak to families whose daughters are out of school. During one of these campaigns, representatives from the organization found me and invited me to a community outreach meeting with other out-of-school girls. At the meeting, the Forum members explained how important education was for our future and urged us to re-enrol in school. They said that when girls go to school, the entire community benefits. Hearing the information they shared gave me the extra push I needed—I resolved to do whatever it took to resume my studies.

To help me re-enrol, the Forum gave me a bicycle to ride from my village to the school in the mornings and back again at night. That bicycle changed my life. The nearest public secondary school is 14-15 km away from my village and it wasn't possible for me to travel nearly 30 km every day to school. My parents were also worried about my safety while travelling the long distance. Hence, I enrolled in a private secondary school 3 km away from my village, which means my journey each day is 6 km in total. That doesn't seem like very much, but there is no transportation connecting my village to the school and the geography of Hamirpur makes the journey on foot very difficult. In the summer, temperatures can climb almost to 50 degrees Celsius! Walking in Hamirpur alone can also be dangerous for girls, especially in the evenings on the way home from school. When I was a primary school student, this difficult journey meant I would often arrive late to class or even miss school entirely. But with the bicycle, I am now a regular student. I attend school daily and arrive on time and I feel safe on my journey back home every night.

Devendra Gandhi, who leads an education non-profit in Hamirpur called the Samarth Foundation, also helped me buy my schoolbooks—something my family could not have purchased. With access to these books, I can study in the evenings when I've returned from school and really apply myself in my studies. This has helped me catch up on the lessons I missed during the year when I was out of school.

After re-enrolling in school, I scored 70 per cent in my board examinations—very good marks for any student of my age. My teachers were very surprised seeing me achieve such a high score despite having been out of school for so long. They were proud of me, but quite surprised at how quickly I caught up after missing out on so much school. My family was equally thrilled about my success.

I am proud of myself too and feel honoured to be seen as a role model in my community. But the best part about being back in school is the very fact that I am here—that I'm once again able to have lunch with my friends, build relationships with my teachers and attend my favourite class, Hindi. This itself is a gift—and one that I hope to bring to other girls in Hamirpur also.

I was fortunate to have parents and brothers who supported my education and helped me overcome the hardships I faced. But many girls in Hamirpur are not so lucky. Where I live, boys and girls are not given equal opportunities when it comes to education. After primary school, parents will spend money to send their sons to private secondary schools but will not do the same for their daughters. This is more of a problem because there are very few public secondary schools in our district. When girls do not receive financial support from their families to attend private secondary schools, it often means the end of their education.

Even when a public school is available in our district, it is located 15 km away from my village, and the cost of secondary school can be a barrier for many families. This was the case for me after my mother fell ill, and it is now true for one of my friends who was compelled to drop out of secondary school because her family cannot afford the fees. Unless the Right to Education Act expands its mandate and makes secondary education free and compulsory and opens up more secondary schools closer to our villages, this will be the reality for many girls in villages across my country.

Until that day comes, I will be working hard to encourage other out-of-school girls in Hamirpur to return to their education like I did. That is why I joined a group of girl advocates with the the Forum and Samarth Foundation who call themselves 'The Malala Girls ' or 'Shiksha Sahelis'. Our responsibility is to spread awareness among our peers about the importance of girls' education and rights and to encourage families in our village to enrol their daughters in school. We do this through awareness campaigns where we go door-to-door in our community to meet with girls individually, hear about their experiences and inspire them to enrol in school. We sometimes speak directly to their parents as well and explain why they should prioritize their daughter's education.

Our group had once heard about a public primary school in Alipura that did not have a functioning toilet for girl students. There was also no drinking water available in the school, which is a mandate under the Right to Education Act. Due to lack of such facilities, girls would often skip school—especially if they were on their periods. After hearing about the situation and speaking to girls who were students at the school, we set up a meeting with the district representative in our village. We explained that the school was violating the Act because it did not have a girls' toilet or adequate drinking water facility. Thanks to our intervention, the school repaired the girls' toilet and installed a hand pump for drinking water. Since then, girls' attendance has been much more regular.

Achievements like these inspire me to continue my work as an advocate. Like my brothers are for me, I want to be the person who any out-of-school girl in my village speaks to for advice. No matter the extent of hardships, I will try to find a solution to help her continue her education. I want her to know that outside of our village and across the world there is a community of girls like her; girls who have faced barriers in their lives but are working together to cross them. With all of us behind her, I know she can finish her education.

When I grow up, I want to be a teacher. My classroom will be a friendly place; I will never scold my students or push them away. As a teacher, my role will not be confined within the four walls of my classroom. I will meet with girls in their communities and inspire them to come to my school. I will teach them what I have learned—subjects like math and Hindi, but also about resilience in the face of hardship. I will be a role model in more ways than one—a girl who completed her education despite barriers and then worked to help others achieve the same feat.

13

Tabitha Willis

UNITED STATES

I FELL in love with the escapism of books at a very early age. Books like *The Magic of Reality* by Richard Dawkins and *Revelation Space* by Alastair Reynolds fueled my curiosity for science and love for creativity. I loved the limitless possibilities stories brought me. I would be inspired by STEM leaders like Mae C. Jemison and Ruth Lloyd, captivated by works of science fiction or awed by books that demonstrated the wonders of science that go into everyday life. Books were a gateway to knowledge, experiences and a world of bountiful possibilities. However, my love of reading and learning never fully translated to the classroom because of the racism and discrimination I experienced by my teachers.

During my K-12 career, I attended eight different schools in the Chicagoland area in search of teachers to meet my educational needs. As a student with speech and hearing complications coupled with learning difficulties, school officials often labelled me as a 'problem child'. As a girl interested in STEM, some educators told me those subjects were strictly for boys; and as a Black student, I had teachers use slurs against me and underestimate my potential.

My challenges in school started from an early age because my brain and my speech weren't aligning. As a result, I thought I was speaking and hearing correctly, but I wasn't. A lot of teachers immediately wrote me off and assumed these difficulties would prevent me from excelling in the classroom. I felt weighed down by their low expectations of me because I knew that I could excel intellectually if given a chance. Instead of being encouraged to become the person I knew I could be, I felt as if I wasn't even given the opportunity to show who I truly was as a student or individual.

I went to speech therapy at local hospitals and the specialists took the time to see my intellectual capabilities. They saw I excelled in math because I didn't need words. They helped identify my impairment, where it comes into play, where I would need additional support and where I would thrive. My dad had them write up a plan for my teachers to support me, which they didn't ever adhere to. But just receiving that validation from them made me realize that I had no limit to anything I wanted to accomplish. The biggest hurdle I had was merely believing in myself enough to go for what I wanted out of life.

However, my issues in the classroom were far from over. I remember while walking into my class in elementary school, I thought that even if I struggled with some of the other subjects, at least math was going to be my thing. That was crushed when I heard my math teacher say, 'All you boys, I know you're going to be really good at math.' I was so confused by that statement. At such a young age, my teachers were already introducing me to the idea that girls weren't as good at STEM subjects. It was puzzling to me because on the one hand my dad was telling me I could do it and I knew I could too, but then my teachers were already enforcing the narrative that science was not for girls.

In high school, racial discrimination persisted. I watched as teachers allowed White students into advanced classes, while they refused to allow Black students and other students of colour to take the same subjects. I had scored in the nineties on all my entrance exams, but still the school administration told me that I wasn't allowed to take honours classes because of where I went to grade school. It made no sense. I had proven my intellectual capabilities in the exams, but still that wasn't enough. The colour of your skin dictated your level of access to school opportunities such as advanced classes, organizations and programmes. They didn't expect much of us and they let it show. Teachers used slurs and underestimated Black students' potential regularly, without regard to the mental toil it would have on those students. A family friend in the year above me was treated so badly that he had to take a leave of absence from school because of the mental health issues he developed due to the discrimination.

Facing barrier after barrier during my K-12 education was exhausting. Whether it was because of my learning challenges, gender or race, I was constantly told I couldn't do things. Fortunately, I was lucky to have a few allies in my corner along the way who helped me believe in myself. Without their strong presence, I don't know what I would have done.

I had an amazing third grade teacher, Mr Williams. He took the time to realize I was good at a lot of these different subjects and would spend time with me after school, something I really needed at that time. He was the first teacher to say, 'Hey, I think you're smart and you can do this.' That was a big turning point for me because it was the first time someone sat down and gave me the support I needed to shine. I knew from that point on that I had the ability to prove doubters wrong.

I also had the unwavering support of my father. He was my advocate from the start. When he saw a school failing to invest in me or noticed me sitting in the corner of a classroom, he'd have me leave that school and try another. Although he worked two jobs to support our family of nine, he converted our small family room into a classroom, refusing to let me fall behind. He taught me advanced math and science, but most importantly he taught me the power of knowledge and to channel the frustration I felt in school into my academic performance. He encouraged me to not only improve my speech but to excel in all aspects of school. My father was the first person to see my potential. At a time when I couldn't advocate for myself, he advocated for me.

It was due to his support that I was able to do well in school. People had underestimated me my whole life, so I had this burning desire to prove them wrong. Due to my speech, hearing complications and learning challenges, reading was a challenge for me. So I would stay up night after night reading, getting better at it and falling in love with books. My passion for science in particular grew in sixth grade when I had an amazing science teacher, Mrs Karwoski. After our first exam, she pulled me aside to tell me that I had scored the highest grade in the class. 'You're really good at this,' she told me. 'Science could be your thing.' So from that moment on, I decided that science was my thing. I became the annoying kid in class raising my hand all the time to ask questions. Mrs Karwoski fostered that love for science in me and told me about all the amazing science institutions in our city of Chicago that had opportunities for students like me.

But when I went to interview for those positions, I felt so unprepared, often being the only person of colour and one of only a handful of female students. I knew that many of the other students applying came from more privileged backgrounds and schools that prepared them for opportunities like this. I felt as if I had a huge disadvantage and that was terrifying. That nagging feeling of not belonging I felt in high school was back in full force, but it didn't stop me from trying.

One of my first positions was with the Field Museum in Chicago, which is a natural history museum that features exhibits on everything from dinosaurs to space. It offers teens opportunities to conduct research, volunteer or intern. I loved teaching groups of younger kids about science and seeing their eyes light up when they realized, 'Woah, science is actually cool.' Helping other kids get excited about science made me love the field even more. I developed amazing friendships with students from across Chicago who were completely different from me— but that didn't mean everything was perfect. As one of a few students of colour in an 80-people programme, I experienced racially motivated microaggressions all the time. Even though we looked nothing alike, people would mix up the few minority girls in the programme. The only other Black girl and I and two Asian students were constantly mixed up and called each other's names. Instead of seeing us as distinct individuals who all had different personalities and contributions, we were seen as outsiders in a community we went above and beyond to belong in.

I knew that the Field Museum and other science institutions on museum campus as a whole needed to do a better job engaging students of colour. That's why I used my position in the museum's Youth Council and Amplify Chicago outreach team to increase the museum's marketing in underrepresented minority neighbourhoods, so that more students of colour would learn about and apply for the museum's STEM programmes. Before I was there, there was no specific outreach to schools with large populations of students of colour. Applications usually came from wealthier students who attended well-funded schools. I made an effort to target students who would benefit from an experience like this the most, who wouldn't have other opportunities like this because of where they lived, their income or other barriers.

As part of my work in the council, I also helped develop a proposal for a programme that took science to the streets through a bus. The bus would have aspects from each of Chicago's science institutions—the science and industry museum, natural history museum, aquarium, Chicago zoo system and space museum— and it would travel to communities of colour and engage students with STEM education projects. There's this perception in many communities that museums are dusty, old and not for young people but they're actually the exact opposite. I wanted to help dismantle those beliefs and show that science is for everyone and the best way to learn more was to engage with the opportunities available to young students in their communities. The museums loved our bus proposal and we're excited to work on bringing it to life now.

For years I've been working to make it easier for the next generation of Black students in Chicago to study STEM—but I can't solve this problem alone. I believe increasing minority access to STEM careers starts in the classroom. Teachers must give Black students the opportunity to see themselves as engineers, scientists, doctors and in more such professions by creating a curriculum that highlights the contributions of the Black community to STEM fields. A lot of the education that I received focused on a Whitewashed history and Whitewashed STEM education. I learned about White people's contributions to different fields and that's it. I think a big step would just be to make our history books and science books more colourful. I want teachers to acknowledge and celebrate the contributions of people of colour to STEM. I want students to be able to study people who look like them. Charles Darwin was great and it's awesome that he created the fundamentals of biology and anthropology, but he couldn't have been any different from me. Ensuring that students are reading about people who look like them and have had some of the same experiences or challenges as them is how we're going to get more students of colour involved in science.

There is also a dire need for companies and institutions to reach out directly to minority institutions of higher education to recruit talented students of colour. It is not enough to encourage diversity if programmes don't take active purposeful steps to bridge the gap placed in our society by institutional racism. Institutions need to think about the barriers preventing students of colour from participating in these opportunities— lack of awareness, transportation concerns, funding, etc.—and address those barriers so that their programmes are truly open to everyone.

Finally, the most important way to increase and maintain diversity in STEM is to listen to Black voices. Understanding and amplifying the experiences of Black students and professionals is the only way we can change the landscape of STEM fields. During my time working at a top scientific institution in Chicago, I was discriminated against by a colleague and had no one to turn to when I wanted to express my concerns. He was very welcoming to everyone on our team, except me. As the only person of colour, I felt targeted on a daily basis. I distinctly remember one incident when he tried to get my attention in a crowded hall. I didn't hear him as I often struggle to align sounds with my brain in noisy surroundings. When I finally noticed, he berated me asking, 'Are you deaf or are you stupid?' At the time I was ignored by an all-White staff who had no desire to try to understand what I experienced as a Black teen under their management. Instead, they insisted that I must have been an aggressive instigator in the situation. My manager had the opportunity to be an ally, but instead she dismissed my experience. With no other people of colour on my team, I felt like no one was there to represent me.

We need to diversify the landscape of STEM to prevent such incidents and from hurting future young students of colour looking to pursue science. I don't want any other students to go through the pitfalls I've had to go through. That's why I work so hard to increase representation and access to STEM in my community. I might be the first person who looks like me in a lot of these spaces, but I'm determined to make sure I'm not the last.

14

Clarisse Alves Rezende

BRAZIL

W HEN I think of Caramuru, my beautiful home, I first think of family—my parents, Moisés and Claudinéia, and my brothers, Vandenilson and Kaiowan. We belong to the Pataxó Hãhãhãe tribe in northeastern Brazil, and this land in Bahia state has been our home for as long as I can remember.

I was three or four years old when my mother first enrolled me in Caramuru's Indigenous school. I've always known that going to school is a privilege and back then, it was a source of joy for me. I loved attending school events and classes with teachers who make lessons dynamic and fun. I loved dancing the Toré, a sacred ritual among my people where we call upon spirits through song in a hut in front of the building, held in a space in front of the building where we celebrate the Enchanted spirits through chants.

But as an Indigenous girl in Brazil, my educational experience hasn't always been a positive one. Since those happy and carefree days at my first Indigenous school, I've experienced many barriers to my education. Like many other Indigenous girls, I've had to fight for my right to learn.

Currently, my family lives in a village that is 15 km away from my high school and our access to public transportation is very limited. Every day, girls in my community make difficult, sometimes dangerous, journeys to get to school. In the mornings, my classmates and I walk several kilometres to a bus stop where a minibus picks us up. Later, we switch to a bigger bus which takes us to our school. The roads in Caramuru are dilapidated and full of holes, so our buses often break down on the way. When that happens we go to school on foot, often arriving so late that we miss our first class. If the bus breaks down far away from school, we have no choice but to go back home. Sometimes this happens on the way back in the evenings, and we are left to walk long distances in the dark. This is dangerous in Caramuru—especially for younger kids.

The conditions in my school are not much better. Our internet connection is not good and the students cannot use it; only teachers and managers are given access. The school has many computers, but they are damaged and do not function. Due to that, we no longer have computer classes at school. In the cafeteria, we have to wait for other people to finish their meal before eating ourselves because there aren't enough dishes, spoons and glasses for everyone. Sometimes, there isn't even enough food. Until last year, even our bathrooms had not been renovated. There was no water to wash our hands with or even toilet paper in the stalls, so students had to use the woods behind the school.

Frustrated by such injustice, I created a group with my cousin and a few other girls in my class to address some of the problems we faced. We first wanted to do something about our school lunches, which were poor in quality and sometimes not enough to feed all the students. We decided to create a petition for our classmates to sign, informing our community about the issue and explaining what improvements needed to be made. With help from our school secretary, we handed the paper to a school board representative and waited for them to call us to a meeting.

But we never saw that paper again. It seemed the school board didn't want us to bring up the subject. When we talked to our school director about it, she explained that our school used to receive money from the government every year to renovate its facilities, but over the past few years the money had stopped coming. To save funds, we shared our lunch with three other schools in the community. It was disappointing that our efforts didn't amount to anything—and even more disappointing to learn that the reason some of our students couldn't eat was because the government wasn't investing enough in our education.

The under-resourcing of my school in Caramuru is part of a larger problem of Brazilian leaders who are hostile towards Indigenous students and indifferent to our problems. There are more than one million out-of-school children in Brazil today, and Indigenous girls face some of the greatest barriers to education. This marginalization of my people has persisted for generations; my grandmother spent her youth as an activist, travelling around

Brazil to defend Indigenous rights and demand improvements for our community. With her as an example, I've been participating in Indigenous rights events all my life. Though I've faced many difficulties as an activist, I am determined to defend my people, to make leaders aware of our experiences and seek improvements for my school.

That is why I work with the Malala Fund-supported organization National Association of Indigenous Action (ANAÍ) to advocate for my people. In November of 2019, I travelled to Brasilia, the capital of Brazil, with ANAÍ and a group of Indigenous and quilombola (descendants of enslaved Africans) girls to participate in a public hearing before the Congress. Through letters and speeches, we urged our leaders to renew the Fund for Maintenance and Development of Basic Education and Valuing Education Professionals (FUNDEB), which is a financing mechanism that the Brazilian government uses to make sure Indigenous and quilombola schools get the resources they need to support their students.

The day before the hearing, the other girls and I did a Toré to ask Encantados (enchanted spirits) for strength and protection. I am a very shy person, so I needed courage to stand up before my leaders and fight for my community. When it was my turn to speak before the Congress, I explained what resources were missing from my school and the difficult reality for Indigenous students in Brazil. I told them that when I graduate, my degree will represent all the days that the school bus broke down and I couldn't make it to school. Or when we went months without teachers because in my state the selection of Indigenous teachers is far from ideal. I will remember the times we had no classrooms to study, when there were no school meals or even water for us to drink.

I also explained how students and teachers at non-Indigenous schools in Brazilian cities are hostile to Indigenous students. In these schools, we often suffer prejudice for being who we are and have to think twice before painting our faces or putting on our headdresses—something absolutely sacred among my people. Many of my Indigenous teachers have told me stories from their time in non-Indigenous schools, how the students there told them that Indigenous people live in bushes and that they shouldn't even be studying.

Participating in this event was very important to me. I felt proud to have been a part of it, to have taken my community with me and fought alongside other Indigenous girls for the rights of our people. I was especially excited to meet Joênia Wapichana, the first Indigenous woman elected to the Brazilian National Congress. Though I felt nervous to speak at first, the girls gave me the courage and strength to talk without shame about the reality of Indigenous schools, what happens to us, how we live and what we go through every day. It was important for parliamentarians, senators and congresswomen to understand our reality, so that they could begin to make improvements—not only for us, but for every Indigenous girl in Brazil.

In August 2020, nine months after our hearing, the Brazilian National Congress approved a constitutional amendment that made FUNDEB permanent. I was really happy when I heard the news. I was proud of our group of girls for going after a goal and winning a victory for our people. But renewing FUNDEB is just the beginning. Meaningful change for Indigenous girls in Brazil requires more work on the part of leaders to meet our demands. It is our leaders' job to ensure we have internet access and functional bathrooms in school. It is their job to fix the roads in Caramuru so that we can commute to school safely. It is also their job to ensure that Indigenous students are safe from discrimination—inside and outside of the walls of our classrooms.

One way they can ensure all that is by ensuring Indigenous girls have access to schools in our own communities, with classes taught by Indigenous teachers. In schools in the city, teachers don't teach us our history. They don't talk about our stories. They care more about *their* experiences, *their* reality; they don't say anything about our own. For example, before I went to school I was always told that Pedro Álvares Cabral had 'discovered' Brazil. But in school in Caramuru, my Indigenous languages teacher explained that Cabral had actually invaded Brazil and taken it by force from Indigenous people. The books I'd read said nothing about this history, they only talked about Cabral. It is very important for Indigenous students to have schools in their villages so that they can learn the correct history and keep its memory alive.

Our leaders must also address the gender inequality that prevents girls from completing their education in many regions of Brazil. Some people believe that girls should not be studying but that a woman's place is at home, cooking food and doing laundry. I've seen some girls in Caramuru drop out of school because they married early or became pregnant very young. To fight this, schools should have better resources to help young women complete their education while raising children, such as appropriate rooms with mattresses where they can keep their children during the day. Teachers should also be informed about these issues so that they can support and encourage their female students to not give up on their studies. My teachers in Caramuru motivate us a lot; they tell us every day to go after what we want and to never give up. It's because of them that no girls in my class have dropped out of school.

I would also like to see the government send resources to our communities that will help Indigenous students experience a variety of classes at school. It is very difficult for us to access projects like handcrafting or computer classes. My brother had to pay for a computer class himself since the computers at our school do not work. Having special courses like these will help Indigenous students enjoy their time in school and prevent more girls from dropping out. It will also help us better prepare for the careers of our choosing.

Most importantly, leaders need to listen to students; to hear what young people have to say about the difficulties we face in our lives every day. We should have the opportunity to participate in meetings with an equal voice, to speak without fear about our experiences and express our ideas for improvements. To girls around the world who are already speaking out, this is my message: As much as there are difficulties in our lives, we must seek the strength to carry on. We cannot give up. So push the barriers out of the way and keep fighting.

I will graduate from my school in Caramuru soon, but I will never leave my community behind. It is with the struggles and achievements of my ancestors that I will earn a law degree one day and continue defending the rights of my people. We will not back down or give up. We will paint the universities with genipapo and urucum. We will dance our Toré in our villages, schools and universities. I will keep fighting until every Indigenous girl is able to receive a quality education and see my people represented in the lessons they learn.

15

Shweta Sharma

INDIA

I'M from an area near the Jaipur railway station after Hasanpura called NBC, in India. A lot of people here are originally from villages, so the place has a rural background in a way.

One of my favourite things here is how open-minded everyone is when it comes to girls and women. There are no restrictions in terms of gender where I live. Girls and women can choose to go out and come back as we please; so my grandmother, my friends and I have the freedom and mobility that I know women in other communities don't have. However, the area isn't safe at night, so there's some restriction in that sense. Most people don't step out of their homes after 10.30 at night. It's not too much of an issue for me because I love my house and since this area is mostly industrial, there aren't food stalls or anything like that nearby

103

anyway. One thing I do like to do before it gets too late is to go to a temple near my house at night. It has a beautiful garden within its complex. I find it really relaxing and comforting.

I am the oldest child in my family with three younger sisters and a brother. Even though I'm older than them, every day I learn something new from them. They're so confident. If someone says something they don't agree with—for instance, that girls should not be stepping outside—my younger siblings will tell them they're wrong and explain why. I want to be more like them and be as straightforward, direct and vocal. My siblings really take after our mother, who is fearless and always chooses to speak out. My mother is my closest confidante and friend. She counsels me through every decision in my life; we share a wonderful relationship. My mother is always supportive of me, particularly of my education. She had to stop studying after twelfth grade, which is why she works very hard to ensure that the same doesn't happen to me.

I was really interested in school from an early age. When I was just two years old, I would pack a bag of books and try to go to school with my aunt's son. Once I officially started my education, my journey wasn't smooth. I attended a lot of different schools and experienced several interruptions.

When I was in upper kindergarten, my parents used to get into terrible fights. It got so bad that my mother had to leave our home and move back to our grandmother's house. I wanted to stay with my mother, so I went along with her. I couldn't go to school there, so my mother worked to educate me from home. She didn't want me to miss out on my studies because of our challenging family situation.

Once I was able to go back to school, I was placed in the fourth grade because I could read and write due to my mother's at-home lessons. But one of the teachers said I couldn't be there because I hadn't completed the earlier classes and that I needed to go to third grade. I had made friends in fourth grade and I knew enough to be there. Moreover, my younger sister was in the third grade and it was embarrassing to have to study in the same grade as her when I knew I should be in an older class. But there was a lot of confusion because I had missed school and exams when I was learning from home, and the teachers were insistent. I was in a state of frustration and anger. I could read, write and study, yet I was being told I should be in a lower grade. My mother tried to come to school and convince the teachers otherwise, but they still made me sit in third grade. As a result of all this and the teachers' refusal to let me be in the grade I should be in, I dropped out of school.

We decided I should go to a school where the teachers are more supportive. During that time I took the admission exam for a local school in Jaipur where I was accepted in the sixth grade, but because of the financial challenges at home, my father was not able to pay the school fees and I had to drop out of school again. After that, my mother helped me study at home and I passed the entrance exams for Neerja Modi, one of Jaipur's biggest schools, and received a scholarship for free education. It seemed like things were on the right track again. However, by then the construction for Jaipur metro had started and there were a lot of strikes happening at that time because of that. This meant that my route to school was closed and because my family couldn't afford a taxi service, I had to leave that school too, halfway through the year. Between Neerja Modi and my previous school, I tried to complete fourth grade three times but never finished it.

These interruptions in my education were frustrating. But it didn't diminish my love for studies. My mother always told me that a woman should be able to stand on her own feet and if she's educated, she doesn't need to ask anyone else for help or money. Education allows women to earn her own money. She told me that people will only respect you if you're educated. My mother made sure I valued education even at a time when my teachers made it hard.

Eventually, I started attending fifth grade classes at a government school close to my house. I wasn't formally enrolled in class, but the principal was very supportive and let me attend. Thanks to her, I got formally admitted to sixth grade. However, at this point, I was a lot older than the other students in class due to the years I had missed out on and the repetition of third grade. My mother thought I should be in eighth or tenth grade by then. The other principal of the school disagreed with my mom and wouldn't let me skip any grades. Finally, my mother talked to someone in another private school and helped me enrol in ninth grade there.

It was an English-medium school, which was very hard for me because everything was in English. I had a hard time with math in particular because I didn't have the strongest foundation after all the classes I had missed. But I was committed. I was determined to complete my education after so many barriers; I stepped up and completed ninth grade.

Anjali, from India, leading a cycle rally for
spreading awareness about girls' education.
Right to Education Forum

Anjali attending a civics class at her school.
Right to Education Forum

Anoyara Khatun receiving an award from
President of India Pranab Mukherjee in 2017.
Save the Children

Anoyara speaking at The Telegraph
She Awards in 2016.
Save the Children

Aramide Kayode, from Nigeria, on her
graduation day at Harvard University in 2021.

Aramide seen here with the students of Talent Mine Academy in Ota in 2021.

Arooj Khalid on a visit to a Montessori in East Lansing, Michigan, US, to talk about her life in Pakistan and introduce the children to her country and culture.

Arooj attending a Model United Nations event at Forman Christian College in 2017.

Arooj on a visit to a high school in Reading, Massachusetts, US. She attended a writing class there and spoke to the students about life in Pakistan.

Youth Journalism International

Charitie Ropati, from the US, standing before the Low Memorial Library of Columbia University, where she is a student.

Houda Hamadi during her first year of medical school in Morocco, 2017.

Husnah Kukundakwe at Hotel Africana in Kampala, Uganda.

Karenjeet Bains, from the UK, competing at the World Championships in Helsingborg, Sweden, in 2019 as the first British Sikh female to represent Great Britain.

Karenjeet at the Commonwealth Powerlifting Championship in 2019, where she won 3 gold and 2 silver medals.

Katiuska Sanchez from Venezuela.
Ivan Jensen

Angelina Tropper from Canada.
Katharina Mertens-Tropper

Rahel Sheferaw from Ethiopia.

Tabitha Willis from the US.

Shweta Sharma studying at her home in Rajasthan, India.

Shereen Kanwal, from Pakistan, giving a presentation on 'Classroom Assessment' at her university, where she is studying to become a teacher.

Shereen in her university hallway.

Nibras Basitkey, from Iraq, on her high school graduation day in the US in 2018.

Nibras speaking at the 'Drive for Five' event at the United Nations in February 2020.

Tamana studying at her school in
Bihar, India.

Tamana with her schoolmates.

Tina, from India, ready to go to school.
Akash Dhaka

Tina at her home in Rajasthan, India.
Akash Dhaka

Once I had successfully completed ninth grade at the English-medium school, I went back to the government school to enrol in tenth grade with the proof that I should be there. My teachers were angry that I had skipped so many classes and had completed ninth grade at another school. But they knew I was a bright student and they didn't want to lose me, so they let me continue my studies there. You see, tenth grade exams matter a lot and the results reflect on the teachers and how well they're doing their job. So I think they let me continue because I could help with the exam scores of my class. Eventually, the teachers started pointing me out as an example. My science teacher used to bring me to the front of the class and say, 'Look at this student. Look at the improvement she has made. She is an inspiration for all of you.'

However, not all my teachers were that supportive. My math teacher used to tell me I would not be able to pass. But my mother told me to study hard and prove that teacher wrong. I did just that and despite all the odds and barriers, I was able to complete twelfth grade.

I wanted to pursue my education further after twelfth grade and was preparing for higher studies. However, I faced more challenges. My family was struggling financially after my grandfather had passed away and my father had lost his job. We couldn't afford for me to continue my education. As a result, I was unable to enrol in college.

I started looking for work that could help me continue my education. My aunt told me about a volunteer opportunity with Restless Development, a Malala Fund-supported organization that supports young people. I started work there as a paid volunteer in Rajasthan, conducting research and interviewing young girls about their experiences. One of the proudest moments of my life was when I received a certificate for my work certifying me as a professional researcher with Girl Effect's TEGA. As a TEGA— or 'Technology Enabled Girl Ambassador'—I speak with other girls to understand their lives and collect what they say on a smartphone using Girl Effect's digital tools. My mother was there when I received it and she told me she had seen a lot of changes in me since I started my work as a research volunteer. She said earlier I was not able to speak up, but now I seem confident in talking to anyone.

One of the most important changes in my life since I joined Restless Development is how I'm now able to pay for college myself using my monthly stipend. College is a lot of work. If anyone tells you college is easy and involves less work than high school, they're lying to you! But I love it. I'm currently in the second year of my bachelor's degree and am also a part of the college badminton team. All this is because I made this opportunity happen for myself. I'm doing just what my mother always wanted me to do: paying for myself and not relying on anyone.

I hope to use my degree to become a social worker and help other girls. I was lucky enough to have a few women in my life who championed my education and made sure I continued to learn. I want to be such a role model for other girls, especially because a lot of girls in India aren't encouraged to go to school or are told that boys are more important than them. I want to tell girls that there will be people who won't believe in them or tell them they can't do something, but that they shouldn't listen to those naysayers. I didn't and look what I was able to accomplish.

16

Aramide Kayode

NIGERIA

I'VE wanted to be a teacher since I was six years old, but teaching is an unusual ambition in my country. In Nigeria, students aspire to be bankers, doctors, accountants or engineers. Nobody wants to be an educator. Young people see teaching as a last resort, the path you choose when all others are closed to you. There were points in my life where I questioned this path because of the negative opinions people in Nigeria have of teaching, but deep down I always knew I wanted to teach.

In primary school, I remember placing bottles of drinks in rows and pretending that they were my students. I wanted to pass on what I was taught in class to anyone or anything that cared to listen. At the time, these bottles played that role. In secondary school I tutored my friends in math, teaching them basic arithmetic and algebra. I hosted my classmates in my room in university to discuss difficult concepts and review assignments. No one paid me—I was doing it because I loved it. I loved seeing my students improve and seeing them thrive in the academic community made me happy. As they invested more in school, their grades went up and this inspired a positive mindset that wasn't there before. Just by teaching, I was helping people become better versions of themselves and it was such a fulfilling feeling.

Eventually, the university registrar appointed me to be an official tutor and I took on my first student—a girl whose failing grades had made her feel different and inferior to her peers. I held tutorials with her twice a week and made our lessons interesting because I wanted her to enjoy the process. I know learning can be a difficult task, but I love to make learning fun for my students. By the time we finished our sessions her lowest grade was a C. I realized that teaching came easily to me and I was good at it. I had just found a talent that I could leverage to make people's lives better.

Before I started teaching professionally, I invested time and effort in first learning about the education system in Nigeria to understand what was happening in my country. As a university student at the time, I didn't know much about the Nigerian education system. In the community where I grew up, all the children went to school so I had never seen anyone roam the streets because they could not afford to go to school. I had never seen the darker side of the system. So I started researching schooling around the world and comparing systems for context.

This was when I learned how our education system was depriving marginalized children of their right to education. There are 13.2 million out-of-school children in Nigeria, many of whom cannot afford tuition. The issue is not only a lack of funding (although that's a big part of it), but also lack of learning quality and standards. The education system is just like a factory that is producing unfinished output. It produces individuals who know the concepts but cannot apply them. This is because there is too much emphasis on standardized testing rather than on how to apply the knowledge practically. Most college and university graduates have to attend additional trainings after their degrees before they are finally fit to work. An education system that is qualitative should create graduates who are prepared for the labour force and are well-equipped with the capabilities required to solve problems and add value to their communities.

Teaching used to be a lucrative profession in Nigeria, but now educators aren't respected or looked up to at all. Even my parents thought I was joking when I said I wanted to teach. There is a perception in Nigeria that teachers are low achievers, people who could not find success in other fields. In universities here, when students are rejected for an accounting or a medicine course, the administration pushes them into studying education. I decided to use my career to correct this notion and to show how much impact people can make in their classrooms and communities when they follow their passion for teaching. Teachers help shape young people into their future selves, allowing them to realize their full potential. I mean, there wouldn't be any doctors, bankers or engineers without teachers.

While at university, I stumbled upon the Teach for Nigeria Fellowship—a two-year leadership development programme where young people are posted to low-income communities to teach. I decided to apply because the increasing number of out-of-school children bothered me a lot and I wanted to join the fight for educational equity in Nigeria. As part of the fellowship, all the fellows had to attend a compulsory six-week summer programme, where we learned basic classroom practices and teaching styles as many of us came from non-teaching backgrounds. Then we got placed in public and low-cost private schools in underserved areas across the country. Even though we were only trained for the basics, I wanted to go deeper. I had learned so much from the six-week training, but I wanted to expand my learning so that I could know more about teaching practice and in turn do more for my kids.

A few months into my fellowship, I realized one thing: our education system is failing the average Nigerian child.

Most of my students had to hawk on the streets after school on a daily basis to help fund their meals, notebooks, textbooks and tuition fees. Many of them do not receive three square meals a day, which led to an increase in malnutrition, sickness, absenteeism and dropout rates. I also saw a problem with the mindsets of my kids. It was difficult for them to invest in their schoolwork because they couldn't see the point of learning as they were influenced by an environment that did not value education. Unlike the community I grew up in, there was nobody in their neighbourhood who woke up at 5 a.m. to go to work in a bank or as a doctor. The quality of education is so poor that even people who had been to school had little or nothing to show for it. My students saw older people in their community roam the streets aimlessly, with no vision or future aspirations. There was no one to look up to and no living proof that paying the yearly school tuition was a smart investment. Parents would rather send their kids to hawk than pay for schooling because they weren't sure if getting an education would benefit them.

One day while teaching, I walked out of my classroom for a break and found a few kids roaming around the streets instead of being in school. When I asked them why they were out on the street, they explained that they couldn't afford the public school education tuition that was 1,200 NGN at the time—about $3 per term (three months). This was a luxury their parents couldn't afford to pay!

When we finished speaking, I asked them if they'd be interested in taking free lessons from me on weekends. If I opened up my classroom, I wondered, would they come every Saturday? They said yes. This was when I discovered that they weren't in school not because they were not interested in learning, but because their parents just didn't have the resources. These are two separate problems: some children can afford education but don't see the value in it, while others want to learn but cannot afford the tuition at all.

I wanted to show these kids that they had a right to education, that learning would do more for them than they or their families could ever imagine or see in their environment. I couldn't understand why any child should be exempted from the transformative power of education. After that encounter, I started teaching groups of students free of cost every Saturday for two to three hours along with other volunteer teachers. We taught them math, English, literacy, computer skills and critical thinking as well as creativity, arts and crafts. To measure our student's progress, we tested them at the beginning and at the end of the programme. Their average score had increased from 25 per cent to 70 per cent! It was clear that our initiative was working. So I thought to myself: why not open a school just for these kids?

Talent Mine Academy, my school for underserved children in Nigeria, began in that classroom and is still in session today. I teach math, English, digital literacy and life skills in Ota, a largely low-income community in southwestern Nigeria. We recently opened another branch of my school in Lagos too. My students range from the ages of six to sixteen; some of them started school at a late age because their parents couldn't afford their education until now. These are children without a voice in our community, and it's a privilege being the voice for them.

I work to change the status quo for my students and other marginalized kids in low-income communities in Nigeria. I mostly raise funds from family and friends to cover the school fees of my pupils and provide notebooks and writing material for them as well. I leverage technology to engage my class and teach them basic digital literacy so that they can participate in the digitally driven world. I teach them skills valued in the twenty-first century job market—like creativity, public speaking, critical thinking and moral values—through puzzles, riddles, art projects, community service initiatives, presentations and group work. I help them see what life is like for their peers around the world by connecting them electronically using the Empatico tool.

But there is only so much I can do when the Nigerian education system is so flawed. My experiences in the classroom over the last few years have taught me a few crucial lessons about what needs to change in the Nigerian education system. To start, we need more trained educators—only two-thirds of teachers have the minimum qualifications. Exacerbating the issue is the shortage of Nigerian teachers in general. The country requires 400,000 more primary school teachers between 2012 and 2030 to meet the demand, and that's not even taking into account the needs of secondary schools.

Addressing the shortage of Nigerian teachers means ending the stigma that bars would-be educators from entering the field. The general notion in Nigeria that teachers are losers creates a cycle: those who are passionate about teaching are dissuaded from pursuing it, and those with no interest in teaching become teachers as a last resort. There are too many people in the system who don't know how to teach, who entered the field because there were no other jobs. They just want to make money and earn a living, irrespective of how they make the children feel. Recruitment strategies in Nigerian schools must become more intentional, with the priority being to hire extremely smart and capable people who can actually handle kids with love and respect and do their job.

To correct Nigeria's education system, the government also needs to invest in more teachers and offer more training for educators at all levels. The standards of the teacher certification should be raised so teachers are better equipped to take on the challenges of leading a classroom. Nigerian schools need to regulate textbooks to ensure they are up-to-date and free of ignorant stereotypes, and also provide training to older teachers whose methods may be obsolete. Teaching twenty-first-century skills is paramount in preparing kids to be active participants in the labour force. When we don't educate our kids with the skills they need to achieve their ambitions, we lose out on the value they can add to our economy in the future.

Furthermore, teachers need to learn how to look after their mental health on the job. As a teacher, I go through emotions alongside my students, whether it's the death of a parent or a house having been burned overnight. When something goes wrong in their lives, it is always a painful and heartbreaking process for me. I remember the day one of my students showed up at my doorstep at 4 a.m. in the morning. She was such a bright child, one of the smartest in my class, and that night she had run away from home without telling anyone. I let her stay the night and walked to school with her the next morning. Her aunt and uncle were waiting for her at school, looking very furious and mad. I watched them withdraw this innocent girl from school and send her back to the rural village where she'd grown up. That was the end of academics for that girl, and there was absolutely nothing I could do about it. Moments like these can be difficult to get through without support, considering the emotional burden they bring. This is why I advise that teachers should pay attention to how their job affects their well-being and care for themselves before they burn out.

One other way to reduce stress in teachers is to provide them with training on how to supplement their income. The average teacher in Nigeria make 20,000 NGN or $52 a month. Compared to the salaries of bankers, doctors and accountants, this pay is really low. Poor pay affects teachers' performance in the classroom and keeps bright people from entering the profession. We need to recognize the essential role teachers play in shaping future generations of leaders and compensate them accordingly.

The government should also ensure that schools are truly free for all students and that there aren't any hidden additional fees for families. A public school tuition of 1,200 NGN sounds cheap, but for some families that is a lot of money. Many people in Nigeria run businesses where they cannot guarantee people will patronize on any given day or week; and they have to first pay for rent, food and debts. They have limited resources to invest in school. Children shouldn't have to hawk in the streets in order to pay for their education; the government should be able to fund public schools at no cost. Nigeria needs to expand the Universal Basic Education (UBE) Act through secondary school, so that students are better prepared for the careers of their choosing.

Every day I am blown away by the intelligence of my students and I know that if they are given access to twelve years of free, safe, quality education, they will be forces to be reckoned with in the future. They are the leaders of tomorrow—we just need to give them the tools they need to thrive.

17

Azka Athar

PAKISTAN

MY name is Azka Athar and I am the daughter of Mr and Mrs M. Tazhir Uddin. As you can see, Athar is not my father's real name. It was a nickname only used by family. I don't know how or why I got it, but I liked it. It sort of clicked with my name and so when time came for me to apply to school when I was three years old, I rather forcefully gave my name as Azka Athar instead of Azka Malik. I guess I'm stubborn about some things because that name stuck and is now my identity.

Now that you know the history of my name, let's move on to introducing my big family comprising my two brothers, two sisters and, of course, my lovely parents. With four siblings around, my childhood was anything but boring. No matter how much we fought with each other, we always had each other's back when we needed it.

Being a middle-class family, we had to compromise on some luxuries growing up, like space and clothing. I spent my childhood living in a two-bedroom apartment. One of my proudest moments growing up was when I was finally old enough to move out of my parents' room to the next room where my three elder siblings slept. Until my sisters got married and moved out of the apartment, I shared a bed and clothes with them. But one thing my father never compromised on was our education. To this day he says, 'My children's education is my life's investment.' And he indeed put in all his assets into our education. No pressure, right?

But as their fourth child, when the time came for me to apply to school, my parents were a little concerned about how they would manage financially. But as they say, true determination and good intention is all you need, and God creates new paths for you. As I was applying to public schools like my siblings had, I learned of a scholarship through my father's office. The scholarship would fully fund two students' education at a well-known private school. It was a long shot, but my parents took me straight to the test centre. The odds ended up being in our favour; I ended up performing very well and was one of the two kids who got the scholarship.

The scholarship included everything from tuition and transportation fees to books and uniforms. I got two uniforms for each season; at one point I had more school uniforms than normal clothes. I was always very aware of the fact that I am the only child in my family who had the luxury of studying in a fancy private school with all the fancy textbooks. It is not like my siblings did not perform well in their studies. In fact, I think they were smarter and braver than I am (I never said that to their faces though). But I felt it was my responsibility to make good use of this opportunity, so I tried my hand at everything that I possibly could at school—including French, which I regretted from the very first class.

Languages were a struggle, whether it be my native Urdu, largely-spoken-at-school English or God-only-knows-how-I-passed French. But what I was able to understand effortlessly were numbers, math, logic and physics. Those subjects were more relatable to everyday life and easier for me to understand. They also helped me connect more with my father as math and physics were his favourite subjects to help me with at home.

I always wanted to pursue a career in biology, but pursuing medicine was a long shot in Pakistan. My real interest was in stem cells and as there are very limited resources in Pakistan for research-based education, I started applying to colleges abroad. I knew I had a good shot at securing a scholarship with my grades. And guess what? I got into a university abroad with a full scholarship.

I had talked through every step of the application process with my father, discussing all the expenses. But when the time came to make a final call and apply for a visa, I realized that my ambitious plans were asking a lot more from my parents than just financial support. In our society, it is not a common practice for parents to send their daughters abroad alone for higher education right after high school. Girls can maybe go for their master's after they get married, but they're usually accompanied by their husbands. I think my parents let me go through the process of applying because deep down they believed that I might not get any scholarship, and there was no way I could go without one. They let me try because they knew I would regret it if I didn't. The moment it started to get all real, I could see the worry on their faces. Back then it felt like my plans were not worth the pain that my parents were going through, so I called it off.

I am still not sure if it were my parents who weren't prepared for me to take that big step of living abroad or was it me who was not prepared to convince them that there was nothing to worry about and that I could do it. Or maybe it was just me who wasn't ready because let's face it, I would barely go out of the house by myself; and to think I was capable of venturing out on my own versus knowing from experience that I can do it are totally different things. It wasn't just a big step for me but also for my parents, so unless all of us were on board with the idea, it was never going to happen. So instead of going abroad, I took a gap year before applying to a university in Pakistan.

Since I had ample time to think about what to do next, I realized I wanted to do something other than medicine, engineering or business—the three most popular degrees that young people in my country apply for, resulting in overly saturated fields. So I applied for architecture. I guess I wished too hard for something different because I did not get into architecture. Instead, I got into my second preference, industrial design.

Industrial design was a very new concept and subject in our country (it still is). It was so new that when I started my degree only two classes had come through the new department before mine. The subject involves designing products for manufacturing through the process of mass production. I knew nothing about art or design beforehand. I didn't have an eye for aesthetics, let alone understand industrial design when I first started. I thought it had to do with either factories or factory buildings and was similar to architecture. Even though it happened by accident, the truth is that I have come to love this field. I like product designing and human interaction design and realize now that all the everyday products around us are designed according to human psychology, behaviour and ergonomics/physiology.

When I started my lessons, I learned there is nothing right or wrong in industrial design—a concept hard to grasp especially for students with a science background. A design either works or it doesn't based on the eye of the beholder; it's all about your perspective. For a person who always found numbers and logic easy, I had a difficult time getting out of that bubble and answering a question as simple as 'Elaborate on your thoughts'. This change of study environment from textbooks gave me a chance to look at things differently and opened my eyes to so many new possibilities the course has opened up for me. This field allows you to work with different mediums and find different inspirations to make designs. Whether you're interested in mobile apps, user research, history or anything else, you can get inspiration from anywhere and your passion will reflect in your work; everyone's work is unique and stands out because it is a reflection of their uniqueness.

With my course, I was learning to keep an open mind and try out new things. That's how I got involved with Formula Student. Formula Student is an international student engineering competition held in the UK, for which students around the world design, build, test and race a formula-style racing car. Typically, the students who competed from my university's team were male engineering and business students. But in 2018, I helped change that with the first all-female team to compete in Formula Student from Pakistan.

I had heard about the competition from an alumnus who had participated in it before. A group of us were interested in the challenge and so we decided to form a team. I should point out that none of us were really car enthusiasts, we were more than just eager students interested in the process of building a car from scratch. For me, the biggest attraction was the idea of working with engineers and designing a car from scratch. I wanted to go back to the same old physics concepts and logic that I used to find easy to understand.

To build our team, we approached friends in other departments as we wanted to have as diverse a team as possible. We started out with a mix of boys and girls on the team, but more number of girls. One by one, the boys in our team ended up dropping out. Maybe they were concerned that they would have to do all the heavy lifting and the girls would just hang out. I'm not sure. But we ended up with an all-female team and, needless to say, we did the heavy lifting ourselves.

The competition is a year-long process of building a team, designing a Formula Student car, making a business model and finally going to the UK to race your car at the main event. I started on the technical team, sitting with engineers, working on the design's calculations and then put those calculations into the 3D models with the help of a mechanical designing software. But I did not stop there. Curious about what everyone was up to, I poked my nose into what my other team members were up to. I wanted to make sure we were able to pull off the project and also because I like managing things. Before I knew it, I became the team lead.

Being the team lead was hard. We were just a team of fifteen students, which shrunk to only ten members when things started getting tough. Every one of us was doing multiple jobs at once, but as the lead, I had more responsibility than I ever imagined having. Between the software work, managing the finances, keeping track of procurements, submitting the competition documents, attending sponsor meetings and resolving internal disputes, my phone was always ringing. It almost felt like I was a successful business woman, but one with no profits in her pocket.

One of the biggest challenges I faced as team lead was securing funding. Competing in Formula Student is expensive. You not only have to pay the huge registration fee, but you also need funding for all the different parts. We didn't have the funding we needed. Pakistan does not have an automotive industry so we didn't have many companies we could approach for resources or monetary support. We began approaching small companies owned by friends or relatives to get small funding.

At the encouragement of our advisor, we decided to turn our all-girl team from a setback (which it seemed like then) to a strength. Our marketing and social media team started promoting us online, celebrating the fact we were an all-girl team. We had named our car Naltar after one of the beautiful mountain peaks in Pakistan, and had named ourselves Team Auj because 'auj' is Urdu for zenith/highest point. Suddenly, bloggers were starting to write about us. We were overwhelmed by people's positive responses to us. It was very encouraging and affirming but at the same time, we did feel responsible to set the right example.

I think this was the point where our parents and families also started taking the project seriously or when they realized how serious we were about it. Even my own father had asked me if we were serious about it and who would make the car and go into the market if there were no boys in our team. It's completely understandable for a parent to be concerned about all of that, but I think it was about time he stopped giving me the benefit of the doubt. This doubt that everyone around us had—of us never making it to the final line for reasons like no prior experience, money nor much time—was the biggest motivation for us that kept us going and trying. In our society, people think it is alright for girls to study STEM as long as girls just stick to books. But we all know STEM is so much more than just textbooks. If more women know that they have a chance of working in the field in STEM, they will be more encouraged to adopt it.

Eventually, our marketing team's efforts also paid off and we captured the attention of the government. We ended up getting very generous support from the Prime Minister's Office and secured the funding we needed with just two months left until the competition. Those two months (May and June) are two of the hottest months of the year in most of Pakistan. Not only that, but Ramadan happens then too, which meant we had to fast. Let's just say we had a new found respect for all the labour force who work in such harsh conditions, climatic and otherwise, while fasting during Ramadan.

After months of hard work, the day finally came when the team and our car travelled to the UK to participate in Formula Student. It was quite overwhelming and daunting to see our team's name in the pit lane of the famous Silverstone race track. Due to not having enough funding and the delay in car parts arriving, we knew that our car could barely run. But we didn't care. We got past the intimidation of being around great teams with amazing cars from all over the world and focused on turning it into a great learning experience. Not only were the other teams supportive and informative, but all the judges were also very encouraging and made sure we got the full experience of learning from all the great works around. Our efforts were also acknowledged with the Spirit of the Event Award!

However, that was not the end. The project did not end with the appreciation award. As much as it was a reward for all the hard work done by the team, we hope that the award and our story will encourage girls and women in our society to go after their dreams and study any subject of their choosing, even if it has been dominated by men so far. A step taken by one woman creates a path for another. I took a step with Team Auj and I can't wait to see what path it opens for the next girl.

18

Anoyara Khatun

INDIA

THERE'S an expression in Bengali, '*Din ana, din khai*'. It means what people earn in a day, they eat that day. I think that captures how a lot of us live in my small village in North 24 Parganas in West Bengal. Most people here work as daily wage labourers in fisheries, barely making enough to support their families. If you don't earn one day, you don't eat that day.

North 24 Parganas is an area with a lot of rivers. It's difficult for anything—fruit, flowers, vegetables—to grow since there's so much saltwater. In addition to all the different rivers, there are also a lot of different communities here—Hindus, Muslims and Christians. All of them have issues with poverty. The families are so big that it's hard to earn enough to feed all the mouths. People end up going to other states to find work.

Despite these challenges, I love my village. I love the games people play in the streets or how when you walk around, you end up talking to everyone. My favourite part about growing up here is the community I am a part of.

I have five siblings, an older brother and four sisters. After my father died when I was five years old, life became very hard. My family struggled for a few years to send me to school; as books and school fees were expensive. It got to a point where they couldn't afford my education anymore. The 2009 Right to Education Act—which guarantees every child in India an entitlement to receive eight years of free education—hadn't been passed then. So at the age of twelve, I had to drop out of school and stay at home.

At home, I didn't do much. So, when one day someone came to my house and offered me a job of taking care of a child for another family, I figured I might as well do it. I couldn't study, so at least I could be a help in supporting my family. It turned out that the job was in Delhi, far away from my family, and it was much more than taking care of that one child. I had to do every single household chore for that family. On top of that, they also treated me horribly and wouldn't let me contact my family; they even tried to throw boiling water on me once. I prayed all the time for someone to come and take me away from that life where every day was hell. I used to think that if I ever get out of there, I would do something to stop this practice that I now know is called human trafficking. No child should be coerced into labour and abused like I was.

After six months, I was rescued by Save the Children and Dhagagia Social Welfare Society (DSWS) and was able to return home to my village. During my time away, a lot had changed.

DSWS had opened a centre in my village to help children who had dropped out of school or who had been forced into early marriage or child labour. They offered six months of educational support and then either helped them enrol back in school or enrol in vocational training. DSWS also created a group of children activists who helped them identify their peers who might be at risk of dropping out or entering into early marriage or child labour. This is because children are the first to know if a friend or a schoolmate of theirs has gone missing.

Even though DSWS helped me return home, I was initially a little suspicious of them. I had a hard time being my normal self once I returned home after having been trafficked. I was angry, agitated and suspicious. But then I heard about DSWS's extensive research into the problems our community faced and how to address those. I heard about how they were teaching people not to be distrustful of vaccines, a big issue in North 24 Parganas. I learned how they were challenging attitudes around child marriage and educating families that just because a girl enters puberty, it does not mean she's ready for marriage. I looked at the great work this organization was doing and all the cases of child abuse I saw around me—and I knew I had to get involved. I remembered how I had felt when I was trafficked and how I had prayed every day for someone to come save me. I wanted to be that saviour for other girls.

As part of the children activist group, we'd go to the house of a child who might be at risk of dropping out, getting trafficked or married early, and speak to that child one by one. We'd try to find out what was going on and if they needed our help. If they did, we'd explain to them or their parents why it was a bad idea and what might happen to them if they went through with it. Most parents don't know the places where the traffickers take the children and the kind of work they are made to do. Many don't know why child marriage is bad. Our group teaches them about these things. We'd ask parents if they cared more about money or their child's health and well-being. Being a part of the group gave me purpose again; it gave me a new reason to live.

I'll never forget one of my first experiences with the group. We were supposed to meet to help a girl who had recently returned after being trafficked but was still at risk of being chased down by the same traffickers. This happened at night and my mother didn't want me to leave the house because she was traumatized after what had happened to me. I realized that if I couldn't convince my own mother that this work was important, I won't be able to convince anyone else. So I told my mother that I needed to do this work because what had happened to me was happening to other girls. I couldn't just stand by and let that happen. My mother understood and let me go.

That night our group gathered together armed with sticks and brooms. We crossed ponds and flooded fields amidst heavy rain. But we caught the culprits and dragged them to the local anganwadi centre, where they were let off after a beating and warning by the sarpanch. We realized then just how much of an impact we could have.

Since then, I've been involved with over eighty children's groups consisting of more than 1,500 children who work as guards against human trafficking in their villages. They are committed to eliminate this social ill. Through these groups, I have helped reunite more than 180 trafficked children with their families, prevented 35 child marriages, rescued 85 children from the clutches of child labour and registered 200 out-of-school children into schools.

Despite all the progress I've made, I still get resistance from people in my community for speaking out as a girl. My relatives and other villagers have sometimes bad-mouthed me to my mother. I have been seen as a negative influence on other children and they have been asked to stay away from me. But working with DSWS and Save the Children gave me the strength I needed to ignore their remarks and focus instead on the changes I could make for other children.

In the years since, I've shared my story in the halls of the UN and with newspapers around the world. I have been nominated for many awards, including the International Children's Peace Prize. Wherever I share my story, I am aware that I carry a huge responsibility—responsibility to stand up not just for myself, but for millions like me in India and around the world. I want to not only be a voice for them, but also want to be a messenger of hope. In my village, in my state, in my country as well as in other parts of the world, there are millions of girls and women who are victims of trafficking and abuse. I want to show them that they are not alone; and that those who were once in their shoes are fighting to end child trafficking and making sure that every child is able to have the childhood they deserve.

19

Charitie Ropati
UNITED STATES

WAQUAA, wiinga yupiuga, yugtuun uguvaa. Camiunga Karianaaq, Alaska.

Hello, I am Yup'ik and Samoan and my native name is Uguvaaq. I am from Kongiganak, Alaska.

Whenever I'm invited to speak anywhere, I always start by introducing myself in my native language, Yup'ik—because it is something my ancestors weren't always able to do.

To those reading, I want you to know that I see you and hear you. I want to thank you for seeing me and recognizing my existence as an Indigenous woman but also as a girl who never saw themselves in what was taught to them.

Women are the backbone of Native society. Everything I am is because of the women who came before me, so to know me, you must know about the matriarchs in my own life. I remember my grandmother teaching me to cut fish for the first time back home in Kong (a.k.a Kongiganak). My hands were shaky as I awkwardly held the ulu to cut parts of the salmon so that it could be hung dry on a rack made of driftwood. After I finished cutting what I could I lifted the salmon towards her and she grinned telling me it looked like shark bait. This is a very fond memory that I have of my grandmother. My grandmother's love was shown in how she taught my siblings and I our traditional ways of life. Her love is stern and serious but also filled with laughter. Her love is chocolate ice cream after eating a bowl of bird soup. She is one of the funniest people I know.

My mother, my grandmother's youngest daughter, was one of the first people in our family to graduate from college. I don't think people understand how hard it can be when you are a first-generation college student until you are actually 'in it'. I saw my mother cross the stage as she received her bachelor's degree when I was eleven years old. That's the happiest I have ever been in my entire life. I remember the nights she would stay up studying for her math classes and then come to the kitchen to help me and my sisters with our own math problems. She spoke to us every morning telling us how important education was, reminding us of our worth and how beautiful we are as Native girls with dreams bigger than the sky and mountains surrounding us. I often think of this and am grateful for my mother, and I think about how she wanted to hear this from her own mother but is now telling her children instead. She is my biggest inspiration. I am who I am because of her. She wanted me to pursue my own dreams, no matter how impossible they seemed and spared no means to do that. 'You owe it to our people,' she would say to my sisters and I. She was the first person who saw me for who I am and recognized my existence.

Often in our communities, the trauma we face is met with silence from our elders because of colonialism. Harold Napoleon, a Yup'ik scholar I always refer to because of his beautifully written work, described how we as youth were told to practice nallunguag, to pretend that serious trauma didn't happen in our own families and communities. My mother was the first to go to college, the first to receive a master's degree, the first to live in Anchorage, away from our ancestral home in Kong, and the first to see me and believe in me.

There are moments you are going to remember your entire life because of the pain they caused. In my freshman year of high school, during a mandatory course for graduation, we were talking about Alaska Native people. When the discussion began, I remember White students saying that my people were all homeless, drunk and defeated.

I wish I had the words I do now. It's still hard for me to talk about that day because those moments don't end there, they follow you like a ghost, haunting you even through college. There are people here who don't understand and maybe never will. As a Native student growing up in Alaska, I never saw myself in the history I learned in school. My teachers would speak of my people as if we solely existed in the past, a mere black and white photo in an outdated textbook. I felt invisible. It felt like parts of me were stolen. I held no sovereignty over my own people's narrative in the classroom. The narrative of Indigenous peoples in secondary education is rooted in colonial tradition that accommodates the needs and intentions of White students. It makes White people feel more comfortable with their history. But in doing so, it contributes to the erasure of Native American identity and their narrative because of historical inaccuracies. To learn a history that refuses to acknowledge your existence as a Native person, whose people have been deeply affected by colonialism is akin to genocide. It is a mechanism of genocide because people forget or pretend as if it didn't happen.

When I was sixteen, I conducted research on this issue. I found that American Indian and Alaska Native students have the lowest graduation rates and highest dropout percentages in the US. The graduation rates of Indigenous students are among the lowest in Alaska, despite the state having the highest percentage of Indigenous K-12 students. In my district, Alaska Native and American Indian students have a graduation rate of 62.88 per cent and the highest rate of dropping out compared to any other demographic.

When Native students don't see themselves in the curriculum that they learn, on a land that was once theirs, they're not going to be as motivated to graduate high school. Why would you want to graduate from an institution that continues to contribute to the erasure of your people? If Alaska Native and American Indian students felt their required classes were culturally relevant and inclusive of the Indigenous perspective, we would be more engaged with our education. This is what I found in my research. We shouldn't have to study in an environment that fails to acknowledge the atrocities Indigenous people have faced.

Western education dehumanizes the narrative of Indigenous people and doesn't acknowledge the resilience and diversity of Native culture. We need to understand the history of those that came before to reconcile what happened in the past and what continues to happen to Indigenous peoples.

With the help of Dr Maria Shaa Williams, Director of the Alaska Studies Department at the University of Alaska Anchorage, and Dr Richard Manning, professor at the University of Canterbury, I developed an accurate and inclusive history sub-curriculum of Indigenous peoples that highlights the atrocities faced by my ancestors and focuses on an Indigenous perspective through readings, videos and movies. I incorporated Alaska Native guest speakers to talk about specific events, including the Alaska Native Claims Settlement Act and the Boarding School Era.

Through my curriculum, I wanted both Native and non-Native students to learn about historical trauma because it is something that Native communities deal with every day and not enough people talk about it. Whenever I write about historical trauma, I reference Harold Napoleon, who specifically writes about how historical trauma manifests in our communities. Napoleon states in his book *Yuuyaraq*: 'The survivors were reinforced in their decision not to talk ... by the missionaries who told them their old beliefs were evil. ... The children were, therefore, led to believe that the ways of their fathers and forefathers were of no value and were evil.'

Our ancestors experienced forced relocations, broken treaties, influenza epidemics, persecution, racism, forced missionization, and so much more. These traumatic experiences forced many of our people to turn to drugs or alcohol to cope and then the cycle repeated with future generations. Native communities' disproportionately high rates of substance abuse, mental health disorders, violence and suicide are the result of the lasting effects of this colonial and historical trauma—and students need to learn this.

But students also need to learn how powerful and resilient Native people are. Through my curriculum, I wanted to celebrate our heritage and our resilience. Despite everything we've faced, we still dance, we sing, we laugh, we smile. We still learn our traditions and go hunting. We were never meant to survive because of colonialism. But we did. We're here. We're here and we're thriving. That in itself is so powerful.

As a student teacher, I felt scared at times because I knew the Native students in my class were going to face a lot of the things I have had to face. It's going to take time for education systems to recognize Indigenous peoples and to include Indigenous scholars, so Native students are still going to experience much of the same discrimination that I did. But I hoped that in my class at least, Native students knew that they mattered and that their voices would be heard. This shouldn't be the reality for us, but it is.

This is the approach I hope every teacher in the US takes. Creating a space where students can dream beyond what they were told to be. I want the school administration and board members to understand that more often than not, the environment cultivated in the classroom is violent for Native students. By failing to understand the legacy of violence and dispossession that happened in the past and continues to happen to Indigenous peoples, they are failing Native students.

I'm proud of the curriculum I developed and the classroom environment I created. In the classes I taught in, I found that the curriculum I made was better, in engagement and accuracy, than the current Alaska studies curriculum based on an interest form taken by the students I taught. My high school implemented my curriculum and I'm currently working to expand it to other schools throughout the district. I hope to see other districts across the country make similar changes.

In the US, it is no longer okay to accept narratives that refuse to acknowledge the history of Indigenous peoples. Educators need to listen to our voices. Native voices need to be amplified, especially when it comes to conversations about what we learn. I want Native youth to feel seen in their classes. If American schools want to better accommodate their Indigenous students, they need to work to indigenize their classes and allow space for kids to dream beyond colonialism.

I often think about what my first memory would have been if my lineage and identity weren't defined by colonialism. What would my world look like if this were my reality? Who would I be? These are things I could never answer nor have the privilege to answer. I am proud of who I am and of where I come from and know now what narrative sovereignty looks like.

I thank my mother and her family. They are the ones who gave me the words and courage to speak of our story of survival and brilliance. I also thank you for reading my story. I believe in you.

20

Tamana

INDIA

MY first day of school was at the age of ten. I remember being so excited to enter the classroom, but soon enough I realized that all the other students were laughing at me because I was much older than them. You see, most children in my village start school at the age of five or six. I didn't because I belong to a Muslim community and the main focus there is on religious education. My community wants its young people to focus on the religious scriptures instead of school curriculum or extracurricular activities.

When I was finally allowed to go to school, I found myself getting bullied by my peers because of my age. I was a joke to them. I was so frustrated and hurt by their treatment and ashamed of the way they kept laughing at me. They were ruining something I had dreamed about for so long; things were so bad that I even thought about dropping out. But somehow, I found the inner strength to ignore them and continue my education.

I was able to go to school for a few years, but then I did have to stop. Even though my mother was supportive of my education, my father was facing a financial crisis and I had to drop out to help support my family and take on more domestic responsibilities at home.

This is not uncommon in my village in Kishanganj district. Gender inequality is a common practice where I live. Families often believe that boys are more important than girls and so they give them much greater preference. This is the mentality and culture where I live. Many girls I know experience this discrimination. They have to prioritize domestic work over their education like I did. Eventually, they are often married off at eighteen or nineteen.

But despite these issues, I love my village. It's a beautiful place. People here are mostly very friendly and nice, apart from the kids who used to bully me. If you ever visit here, you'd find a peaceful, kind community living a simple way of life. You might also get impressed with the beauty of my village. We're surrounded by incredible natural flora and fauna. Looking at the natural wonder all around is my favourite part of living here. I also love looking at various designs of the houses and structures of my village when I play with my friends in the evening.

After I left school, I took on greater responsibility at home to help out my parents. I was in charge of cooking, washing utensils and grooming horses. I also had to work in the fields and feed our animals. I was happy to help my parents, but I missed school.

In 2019, my life changed when I met a local teacher with the Azad India Foundation, an organization supported by Malala Fund that helps girls in Bihar re-enrol in school. This teacher heard that I had dropped out to help my family at home and came to tell me that they were opening up a centre for out-of-school girls to learn and receive free formal education.

It sounded amazing, but my parents were hesitant. They were worried about sending me to this place they didn't know. As daily wage labourers, they don't make a lot of money, and were concerned about the expenses of allowing me to continue my education. So they didn't allow me to go. But I couldn't miss out on this opportunity, and so I started going to the centre without them knowing.

With about forty other girls in the village, I started attending the Azad India Foundation centre. I was able to read, study and mingle with friends. Eventually, my parents found out and realized that it was true that there would be no fees for me to attend. They decided to let me continue going. I started to learn English and mathematics there. Before the centre, I didn't understand the connections between school and everything else in life. I didn't realize that what you learn in school prepares you with the skills and knowledge to do other things with your life. And if you don't go to school, you have a lot less opportunities. My education took on a new level of meaning and importance.

With help from the centre, I was able to re-enrol back in primary school. I am currently in ninth grade, and hope to become a teacher one day. My favourite subject is Hindi because it's easy to communicate and understand. I like that we read good stories in class that have moral lessons.

I've also started work as a peer educator. As a peer educator, I help the teacher in the classroom with the younger students. I also go door to door in my village and try to convince other out-of-school girls and their families to allow them to attend school.

Sometimes the conversations are difficult. There are a lot of girls who are not in school like I was. But the fact that I was once in their shoes is my biggest strength as a peer educator. I use myself as an example to both girls and their parents. I say that I used to not do anything or know anything. I couldn't read Hindi or English, I couldn't do mathematics or any subject really. Then I started attending the centre and I began to learn. Now I'm in ninth grade, learning and doing all these incredible things. I help parents see that if I can go from being out of school to becoming a successful student, their daughters can too. 'Why can't your daughters come to the classroom and learn?' I ask. I have to think quickly because not every argument has the same impact on every person. I have to try out different tactics. But it's the best feeling in the world when I'm able to convince another parent and another girl to go to school.

My work as a peer educator is so important to me. I see a lot of gender inequality around me and I want to change it. If boys are allowed to have all kinds of opportunities, if they're allowed to go to school and achieve their ambitions in life, why can't girls? Girls have the same abilities as boys, they are just as capable as being a doctor or police inspector. They just lack the opportunities to do all these things and realize their full potential.

I hope to become a teacher one day so that I can help every girl continue their education. I want to change the attitude toward girls in my village and have people acknowledge our importance and what we're capable of achieving.

21

Karenjeet Kaur Bains
UNITED KINGDOM

IT is June 2019 and I am getting ready to go on stage for one of the biggest moments in my powerlifting career so far: the World Classic Powerlifting Championships in Helsingborg, Sweden, where I am to make my debut representing Great Britain. My head and heart are pounding. Deep breath in ... deep breath out. I recite the lyrics to Eminem's 'Lose Yourself' in my head to calm my nerves. 'You only get one shot, do not miss your chance to blow. This opportunity comes once in a lifetime.' The scoreboard is flashing the names of the strongest lifters around the world and then suddenly I hear the announcer say, 'Karenjeet Kaur Bains GBR, 140 kg on the bar ... bar loaded.'

As I walk forward to take my final squat, the Great Britain national coach gives me a powerful last slap on my back, flicking the switch in my head to my competition mode—aggressive yet focused. I glance up into the crowd and see my father, my coach. My mother, brothers and sister-in-law are next to him. I'll never forget the look on my family's faces as they watched me become the first Sikh woman to represent Great Britain on the international powerlifting stage. That day wasn't just for me, it was for them. Looking back on my journey, I know my strength and success is all because of them.

My family has a knack for standing out, so it was only fitting that I made a dramatic entrance into the world, born to thunder and lightning on a hot summer night in late July, 1996. My father Kuldip Singh Bains was a former competitive bodybuilder and powerlifter. My mother Manjit Kaur Bains comes from a family of wrestling champions. My twin older brothers Parminder and Pardeep Singh Bains are talented football players and national-level 400 metre hurdlers. It quickly became clear to me that my family was full of champions, and that I would one day have to achieve something special to continue the trend.

From an early age, I knew the difference between winning and losing. I've always had an extremely competitive nature. Perhaps it was a futile attempt to keep up with my older brothers, but it worked out well in the end. From this competitive drive to win, I learnt the importance of hard work—a lesson I applied as a student to both sports and academics.

Often at school I found it hard to fit in because I was the studious and sporting student combined. I have always had a thorough appreciation for education; in my eyes, knowledge is power. My parents have always taught us that the most valuable gift you can give someone is a good education because it opens doors to their future. In secondary school, I was head girl at my school for three consecutive years, while also achieving one of the highest scores in my exams in both state and private schools in the county (I owe that success to plastering my brother Parminder's exam results on my bedroom wall as a reminder of the target to beat! Did I mention I was competitive?). I was also the fastest girl at my school, holding school records in the 100 metres, 200 metres and long jump. At the same time, I enjoyed expressing myself through painting and my artwork was often put up in local exhibitions. I was also a keen freestyle solo Bollywood dancer performing at the school talent show. My peers made many attempts to try and crush my confidence because of their jealousy of my skills in and out of the classroom. They would often make me feel like an outsider, never part of the 'popular' circle of friends. They made comments about me in the hallway or talked about me on social media. Despite all their efforts, I never succumbed to peer pressure of trying to fit in. I was not afraid to walk alone as I held my morals and values of being both a Sikh and a sportswoman in high regard. I'm thankful to my family for never letting those seeds of doubt grow. They celebrated me and all my passions, refusing to let me be defined by just one aspect of me.

No matter what I did, my family was there to show their support. At every race, strategically placed on each bend of the 400 metre, I would always hear their four distinct voices among the roaring crowd. My two older brothers would be living and breathing each stride I took. My father would be assessing my race with laser-like precision, stopwatch in hand to see if I had hit a new personal best. The final and most distinct shout of encouragement would come from my mother. Seeing me winning in life meant everything to her. I was living and breathing the dreams she had always had for herself. It always makes me wonder what she herself would have accomplished if she had been given the same opportunities and environment I had as a child.

My mother was born in rural Punjab in the 1970s in a village called Bahadurpur. As a child, she would often wake up at the crack of dawn to help her sisters complete the morning chores before school. She came from a family of farmers, who expected her to pitch in feeding the livestock, milking the water buffaloes and completing the housework as part of the morning routine before school. My mum's mind is extremely sharp and I have no trouble believing it when she says she was an attentive child, eager to learn. She told me that she would try and read any piece of paper she could get her hands on just so she could practice her English, even if that meant delaying the chores and getting in trouble with her sisters. But my mum's dreams of continuing her education like her brothers stopped at the age of twelve when her family told her she had to leave school to join her sisters working full-time in the fields and tending to the farm. My mum was heartbroken and vowed that if she ever had a daughter of her own, that girl would never be denied her freedom.

At the age of nineteen, my mother came to the UK to marry my father who had settled here as a child. Although it was daunting to be in a foreign land where she didn't speak the language, it gave her a sense of hope that this fresh start would finally give her the freedom to pursue her ambitions. After my brothers were born and started going to school, my mother was drawn to their textbooks, remembering her younger self doing the same thing fifteen years earlier. That was all it took to ignite the spark that had once been forced to dim. She would sit with my brothers as they did their schoolwork, taking the opportunity to learn alongside them. Since she had the support of her husband, my mother soon realized that she was no longer bound by any perceived limitations that had once been imposed on her. She seized the opportunity and flew, attending college to further develop her English, becoming fully literate in a once unknown language and obtaining qualifications to suit. That little girl who was once denied her right to learn would have been beaming with pride if she had known what the future had in store for her. But my mum didn't stop there.

There had always been a glint in my mother's eyes whenever it came to sport, you could almost see her eyes light up as she watched her children succeed in the sporting arena. Her apparent curiosity was noticed by my father, who whilst training in the home gym would always be amazed at his wife's ability to pick up heavy dumbbells. To her it was nothing more than simply assessing the weight, but what he saw was undiscovered talent without any formal training. It must have been all the natural strength she had gained during her childhood from years of manual labour, working in the fields as a proud farmer's daughter.

My mum was nervous at first, worried about what other people would say about a middle-aged Indian woman becoming an athlete. But it was now time for her to live life for herself; she didn't have to worry about her family's approval and because her kids had grown up, her child rearing responsibilities were over. So she became a competitive athlete. My proudest moment was watching her bring home five gold medals and four silver medals at the Warwickshire Athletics Championships, a record-breaking medal haul. She looked like a gladiator whirling the hammer in that competition.

People like to say that my strength must have come from my father, the former powerlifter and bodybuilder, but now you know that my power comes from both my parents. Although I pursued track and field as a student, I was always drawn to lifting weights. As a child I would watch my dad and brothers train in our home gym that my dad had created with his own hands. They even installed a homemade swing in the gym for me to perch myself on as I watched them in awe.

If it had been up to me, I would have started lifting weights at a slightly earlier age of say fifteen years. But my parents wanted to give me every chance to grow to my full height, which didn't end up being too tall given I'm 5 feet 4 inches! I first picked up a dumbbell at the age of seventeen, having never lifted before. After having only trained for three months, my father, who was now my powerlifting coach, made me enter a competition. I remember walking into the arena flanked by my strong-looking twin brothers. The referee approached us and asked my brothers if they were looking to compete today. My brothers told him that they weren't, I was. Hearing that made me even more determined to show that I, as a woman, was more than able to hold her own and compete in a stereotypically male sport. It was important to me to show that women no longer had to watch on the sidelines or stand in the background. It was our time to come forward and that day a demonstration was needed. I went on to win that day.

It wasn't the last time I'd win a competition—nor was it the last time I was underestimated because of my gender and how I look. When I was eighteen, my father decided to take me to the place where his love for bodybuilding and powerlifting started, an old gym in our hometown where he used to train. As I set foot into that gym, I was immediately hit by a testosterone-filled environment; there was not another woman in sight. The vibe had changed dramatically since my dad had left; it had gone from a group of committed powerlifters to seemingly intimidating males each aiming to exert their dominance. Despite these attitudes, I stood next to my dad ready to train. A reassuring glance from him was all I needed as I began to warm up heading over straight to the deadlifting platform.

I remember feeling the eyes of the room descend upon me as they saw this slender, petite female invading their space. I kept my head down working on my mobility as my dad began to set up my warm-up weights. Then I felt someone approaching us. One of the more established members of the gym addressed my dad—not me—almost mockingly and told him with regret that this was probably not a suitable gym for women, and that he wasn't sure if there would be dumbbells that would be small enough for me. My dad, my coach and advocate, responded that he wasn't sure if there were dumbbells big enough for me.

Safe to say that first heavy deadlift session immediately silenced anyone else in the gym. Pound for pound, I was the strongest lifter in the gym when comparing the ratio of my bodyweight to what I could lift compared to any male standing there. Little did they know I was the British champion at the time, so it must have been a very humbling experience for them. As they say, actions speak louder than words! I walked out of that gym with the respect I should have received when I first set foot in it. The day those men assumed that I wasn't capable and underestimated me based on the fact I was a girl, ignited a fire in me I didn't even realize I had.

My powerlifting career continued to grow, while I also managed to land myself a scholarship with a top accounting firm. They would pay for my university degree, give me full-time job training to become a Chartered Accountant as well as pay for my ACA Professional Qualification exams. Everything in my life seemed on track. And then suddenly it wasn't. In 2016, I unexpectedly lost one of my best friends and sustained a devastating injury to my piriformis muscle (damage to the hip/glute on my left side). Not only did I have to reckon with the sudden death of an important person in my life, but I also had to contend with the possibility of never being able to lift again. If that wasn't enough, I was also having some troubles with my scholarship. The balancing of work, professional exams and lifting coupled with the tragedy that had just struck in my personal life was all too much for me. To say I felt the weight of the world on my shoulders is a serious understatement.

All of this happening at once felt like I had been hit by a ton of bricks; I was thrown into a deep, dark place mentally, a side of sport that is often not talked about. The highs I had experienced not so long ago had all come crashing down. Both my sport and professional life seemed to be falling apart. I was only nineteen years old, but it felt like everything was ending. This was not how I wanted to be remembered, as a one-off international athlete who had so much 'potential' before she lost it all.

The months that followed were some of the hardest I had ever experienced. I remember sitting in the living room staring at the clock, tick past my usual training time. I sat there with my head in my hands, distraught by the fact that my body was no longer cooperating with me. Every time I tried to lift, I would trigger my injury. My dad walked in and he could see the tears welling up in my eyes. He felt my pain—the whole family did. I was a shell of myself. Lifting had always been an outlet for me to release the stress and anger I had at the world, but now I just sat with it building up inside of me.

I felt a hand on my shoulder as my dad looked me in the eye and said the words I will never forget, 'Karen, you are like the phoenix. You rise from the ashes bigger and stronger than ever.' Even though I was losing every sense of hope, yet here was my dad believing in me as he always did, refusing to give up on me and my future. In that moment, I started to rekindle my passion for powerlifting, which was just a mere ember at that point. It was time to stop feeling sorry for myself. As they say, a setback in life gives way for a greater comeback! Little did I know that it would take me two whole years to fully rehabilitate this injury. I underwent ultrasound treatment, gruelling physio, constant drilling and stretching. There were times I couldn't seem to find the light at the end of the tunnel, but I held on to that one shred of hope that this would all be worth it in the end. I had to start from the beginning; I resumed training with the empty 20 kg bar, forcing myself to leave my ego at the door. Only once I could squat or deadlift the bar without being in pain was I granted the permission to move up to the next weight.

As a former athlete who had competed at the highest level of the sport, you can imagine not only the physical but the mental agony I endured. It took a lot of mental strength to no longer fear the weights and approach them with the same ferocity I once did, willing myself to 'forget' my injury and ignite the Karen I once was.

Come the 2018-19 competitive season, I decided it was time to brave the platform again and enter local competitions. My former fearlessness as an international athlete seemed like a distant memory. Slowly but surely, I built up my confidence again going from county level to university championships, to the All-England championships and finally the British championships. Until one day, a letter came through the door from the Great British Powerlifting Federation saying that I had been selected to represent Great Britain at the World Championships in Helsingborg, Sweden! I could not contain my emotions as I told my family about it. Their eyes were beaming with pride because they knew how much hard work went into that accomplishment, how I had achieved what we once thought was impossible. It was a defining moment especially with my dad. 'WE DID IT!' was all I exclaimed as I jumped into his arms. All those years of doubt, pain and tears were worth it.

Receiving that recognition from the Great Britain team was the sign I needed to start believing in myself once again. Just like my father had said, I was like a phoenix rising from the ashes. Reflecting now on the whole experience, I am almost grateful. As horrendous as it was, time out from competitive sport with my injury ensured I developed mental as well as physical fortitude. If

I could give one piece of advice to anyone out there who might be going through a really difficult time and is afraid that they have lost all hope, I would say: Never be afraid of starting over. This time you are not starting from scratch, you are starting from experience. I finally understand that in order for my body to serve me, be it in my sport or professional career, I had to take care of it and nourish it. Countless hours must be dedicated towards perfecting your craft, educating yourself and honing your skills.

This new driven work ethic I had developed throughout my time away from competitive sport was something I also applied to my academics. Whilst preparing for the World Championships, I was also in the midst of completing my final year at Durham University where I was pursuing a bachelor's in accounting. I later came to learn that I had achieved the highest honours in my degree! Not only that, but recently I also became a fully qualified chartered accountant, successfully passing all fifteen exams—and I did this alongside my professional powerlifting career.

The year 2019 was a transformative year for me as an athlete and an individual. I had emerged from the darkness as a technically sound and much more knowledgeable athlete. I achieved some of my greatest ambitions in powerlifting to date. I officially became the first British Sikh woman to represent Great Britain in both World and European championships, placed among the top ten strongest females in the world of my age and weight. My strongest lifts were a 140 kg squat, a 82.5 kg bench press and a 167.5 kg deadlift—and don't forget that only one year prior I was solely lifting the bar.

But I haven't got to the pinnacle of my story yet. In September 2019, I became the Commonwealth Champion in St. John's,

Canada—my first international title so far! I won three gold medals in the squat, deadlift and overall 63 kg women's class as well as two silver medals in the bench press and bench press-only events. These accolades were even sweeter because I shared them with my family, the four people who had stood by my side throughout this rollercoaster journey of life. Those medals were for my mother who had overcome so much adversity to get to where she was today, for my brothers who have been my heroes from a young age and most of all, for my coach, my father.

Looking down at those gold medals around my neck was one of the happiest moments of my life. As I looked at my reflection in them, I caught a glimpse of a younger version of myself beaming with pride. To me, she represented all the children who had hopes and dreams but did not have the confidence to pursue them. For a split second, I felt the urge to place a hand on that little girl's shoulder, like my father has done so many times, and tell her: You're stronger than you think you are.

22

Manisha Bharti

INDIA

A S a Dalit girl growing up in Kushinagar, Uttar Pradesh, I'm no stranger to discrimination. I'm used to being underestimated or judged based on my gender or caste. But when people ridicule me or my studies, I don't listen. I become stronger.

I want to become a teacher one day and I know that education is the only path to realizing that dream. I also know that I'm not alone in this fight, but have the support of my parents who always encourage me and support my studies. Moreover, I have the example of Baba Saheb Dr Bhimrao Ambedkar—a Dalit leader and the father of Indian Constitution—to look up to as a source of inspiration.

What also motivates me is knowing that girls and women can achieve everything boys and men can. In our country, we have seen women reach great positions of power, walking shoulder to shoulder with men. I want to be just like them one day.

Most people in my community are uneducated and work as daily wage labourers. When I go out in our community, I see women and men engaged in wage work or household work. I see children playing. I see some children working in the agricultural fields. I see girls planting paddies, hoeing, sowing, harvesting wheat and storing grains. There's a lot of poverty and not enough cultivable land where I live, so a number of people migrate to other cities because they can't find employment in the village. This poverty prevents a majority of people from studying. We also have to face caste discrimination and people of other communities physically abusing or sexually harassing Dalit women from my community.

Even though it has its issues, I like my village very much. I was born here, so I will always have an emotional connection with this place. I love going outside and playing with other children. But what I love the most is my family. I have two sisters and one brother. My brother does stitching work outside the home, while my parents work as labourers. I also have to go to work in the fields with my parents because of the difficulty in managing expenses of the house.

My parents have always felt it necessary to send me to school because they didn't want their daughter to be illiterate like them. They don't want me to spend my life working in someone else's field, they want me to think about the future and prosper.

Education has always been very important to me too. I believe that we can only develop as individuals through learning.

This attitude toward girls' education isn't common in our village, however. There's a lot of discrimination between girls and boys. Our community thinks that there's no benefit in teaching girls and that they're inferior to boys. One of the main reasons why girls from the community do not complete their education and drop out instead is our patriarchal society and the gender discrimination in it.

As a Dalit girl, I have also faced caste discrimination in school and been shamed for it. Since there's no government school in our village after eighth grade, we have to commute to a school that's very far away from our homes. As I mentioned, Dalit girls and women face increasing rates of sexual violence. If something happens to a girl while she walks to school, if she's attacked or harassed, other parents hesitate to send their daughters to school as well and this causes even more girls to drop out.

I feel very sad when I see girls drop out. It seems like when a girl studies, not only does she succeed, but her family succeeds as well. Why wouldn't everyone want that for their daughters and themselves? But many parents don't seem to realize the benefits of educating girls. They don't see that when a girl leaves school, her future becomes bleak and that she will never be able to stand on her own feet.

I know how it feels when you drop out of school because I too once had to. I had passed high school and gotten accepted into Mahatma Gandhi Inter College, but in the twelfth grade it became too expensive for us. I had been worried for some time that it might happen, wondering how I would be able to study further and complete the next class. So even though I wasn't surprised when my family could not afford Rs 6,000 that I needed for my admission, I was still disappointed. I knew that my parents really wanted me to study but between supporting me, my sisters and brother, they couldn't afford the education and upbringing for all of us.

My studies stopped then and so, it felt, did my life. I was so sad. But I did not give up on my dream of completing my studies one day. As I worked in the fields with my parents, I collected money for my studies. I was saving up so that I could pay my tuition fees myself.

It was around that time that the Malala Fund-supported organization Samudaik Kalyan Evam Vikas Sansthan (SKVS) came to my village to help students who had dropped out of school to re-enrol again. SKVS held a meeting for out-of-school girls in our village that I went to. The SKVS team connected me to Kishori Sangathan and spoke to me about the importance of education. They discussed the same with my parents too and told them they'd help me get readmitted to school.

Two years after I dropped out of school, I enrolled again. I was so happy knowing that I would be able to complete my education and fulfill my dreams. However, two years was a big gap in my education and it was a challenge to start my studies again. I found it very hard to complete the course. In addition to my academic challenges, I also had social challenges. All my friends had already graduated and I found it difficult to make new friends.

But I'm still so happy to be in school. My life and my future are back on track. My favourite subject is Hindi because it is my mother tongue, I love to talk in Hindi. I recently had a chance to participate in the kabaddi competition where our team won the second position. I was very proud when we got the prize.

I also feel proud that there have not been as many girls dropping out of school in our village because of SKVS and that people have started to understand the importance of education. Many people know now that girls' education is a right. Due to my example and my courage, many other girls in the village have been inspired to start their studies.

I wish there was better, permanent support from the government to support the education of girls like me. It is the right of every girl to be able to go to school, but the government isn't doing enough to help us. There should be more girls' schools in my community so that girls don't have to travel so far or worry about harassment along the way. If there is a school near our village, no girls will drop out. All girls will study and there will be no fear of harassment and sexual violence along the way to school.

Additionally, the government should also make sure that education isn't so expensive. The costs of tuition, study material and commute are difficult for poor families to afford. I've seen how these expenses make a difference for girls when choosing between a life with or without education.

Finally, we need to change the mindset of communities in India that mock girls' education and don't see its value. We need more parents to be like mine, who support their daughters' dreams. Educated girls create a better society for everyone and more people need to know this.

I plan to create a change for girls' education in my community through my future work as a teacher. I want to teach girls and support them. I want to make sure they understand the benefits of education not only in their own lives, but for their family and their community. I want to make them aware about gender and caste discrimination. I want to create a classroom environment that provides equal opportunities for everyone.

23

Houda Hamdaoui

MOROCCO

THE French writer and novelist Albert Camus once said: 'Being different is neither a good or a bad thing. It simply means that you are brave enough to be yourself.'

I must begin my story with that quote because it captures me and my life so well. My family and community in Morocco have always seen me as the odd one. My outspoken nature and determination to express my opinion and defend what I think is right have made me stand out for as long as I can remember. It took me years and plenty of courage to finally realize that there's no harm in being different. On the contrary, it only brings beauty and variety to a world where everything seems to look alike.

One of the things that always made me different was my dream to become a doctor. It's been my goal for as far back in my memories as I can go. At the age of four, I remember playing with my sisters and friends and requesting to play the doctor. This burning need to pursue a career in medicine probably started from the hours I spent in hospital in my childhood. I suffered from several chronic illnesses as a child, so I was often around doctors. I would admire those angels in their white coats who were helping me get better and get back to my life. It was then that I developed an unconditional love for the profession. But at the time, this was a path not many women in my country chose because our society assumes men are superior and that prestigious careers like medicine are only for them. I'm glad to see that changing and now there are more women in my field, but when I was younger, it made me stand out.

My passion grew bigger when I started learning STEM in school and fell in love with biology and mathematics. I realized that I wanted to become a woman of science. I remember excelling in all my school subjects, even the ones considered boring by most of my peers like history and geography. I never thought that anything I learned was boring in any possible way. I loved learning. As a girl, I wasn't allowed to go out and see the world or even dream of travelling because it's not something a girl in my family would do. But because I was lucky enough to be able to go to school, I was able to discover new places and new dimensions that I wouldn't be able to see otherwise.

As I got older, my dream of going to medical school became less hypothetical and more realistic. I studied hard to get the grades I needed. I would prepare for my exams weeks ahead because I wanted to make sure to get the highest marks possible. My focus was mostly on the science subjects. It wasn't that much of a problem for me because I loved studying no matter how tiring and exhausting it was, especially mathematics. The only challenge I encountered was in the form of my senior year mathematics teacher.

I don't know why he was highly triggered by my existence, but he was. Maybe it was because I was outspoken or maybe because I was a girl and was good at the subject he taught. I don't know. He used to give me the hardest exercises and equations to solve before the entire classroom, hoping I'd fail and humiliate myself in front of my peers. I rarely failed though, which made him even angrier.

One day, this teacher asked me what I wanted to do when I was older. I told him I was aiming to go to medical school to become a doctor. He exploded with laughter. 'You know, someone like you will never make it to med school,' he said. 'I've had students a hundred times better than you, who still didn't manage to do it. You should consider a plan B because you're more likely to fail.' To which I answered, 'If I fail, I'll throw myself off a balcony.' And he answered in a tone full of sarcasm, 'If you succeed, I'll throw myself off a balcony.' Don't worry, no one ended up throwing themselves off a balcony, but I did take what he said as one of my biggest motivations to make it to medical school. I wanted to see the disappointment on his face and prove him wrong. Nobody has the right to underestimate you or reduce you to nothing more than what their expectations are of you. Whenever someone does this, my advice is don't take it to heart or feel bad about yourself. Instead, take it as a challenge to bring the best out of you.

And guess what? After a lot of hard work and endless nights of studying, I did make it to medical school. Regardless of how difficult it was, I did it. I did it for myself and to prove those who doubted me wrong. But I also did it for all those who believed in me—especially my mom. It would be so ungrateful of me to not mention her, the person to whom I owe not only this accomplishment but also everything else I have achieved in my life. No matter how delusional my dreams might have seemed, she always believed in me and supported me with everything she had, both emotionally and physically. She has been more than my biggest supporter, she has also been my biggest role model. She's the first woman in her family to earn a PhD. She knew how important education is and how much it can change a girl's life, so she did everything she could to guarantee her three daughters' access to education.

My first two years of medical school went very smoothly. It was all new and exciting, albeit a little bit terrifying. My studies were considerably complicated. One of the subjects that gave me a hard time initially was physiology, which basically explains the way different organs and systems work. The reason why I hated it at first is the complexity of every mechanism. For instance, did you know that the biggest and heaviest organ in the human body is the skin? But I learned to love the subject after realizing how fascinating the human body is and how much of a miracle we all are.

In my third year, I started doing real shifts in the university's hospital. Unfortunately, my experience wasn't anything like what I had seen on *Grey's Anatomy* or *House*. Growing up, I remember watching these series and picturing myself as the main character, saving people's lives, doing extremely complicated surgery perfectly and earning the respect of my peers. Well, you know what? You don't get that in real life. In a country like Morocco, you're lucky to find the basic necessities in every hospital. And everything about the job is harder when you're a woman in a country that discriminates against you for your gender.

After being in the operating room and witnessing the magic of surgery, I decided I wanted to become a surgeon. It is the most incredible experience seeing how the surgeon cuts the patient open and fixes him. The patient wakes up and starts recovering and getting back to his normal life as if he never went through anything. I was super excited to share my ambition with an attending resident when he asked me about which specialty I was aiming to choose. But I was so deeply disappointed when he replied that as future wives and mothers, women should adjust their careers accordingly. Busy, important careers like surgery are only for men, he told me. That is a common mentality in my country. Even if you're highly educated, if you are a woman, you will always be seen as nothing more than a housekeeper and a procreation machine.

It made me furious to be underestimated, but it also motivated me to do my best and show him what women like me are capable of. Over the years, I've been told that I couldn't do something because of my gender more times than I can remember. What I've learned is that you know your potential better than anyone else. Don't ever let someone reduce you to nothing more than a procreation machine and a pleasure tool. Use the most effective weapon at your disposal—your education—and use it to change the world and the mindset around you. I proved my math teacher wrong all those years ago and I plan to prove that attending resident wrong the same way.

Another obstacle I faced on the job was the fact that most of my patients—especially the women—were illiterate. As a student, one of my first tasks was to take the patient's personal information, find out their medical history and write down a possible diagnosis. When I asked my female patients their age, I was often met with the response, 'I'm sorry, I don't know I never went to school.' Or even when I asked them to tell me more precisely about their pain, they kept on apologizing and saying that they don't have the right words for it because their vocabulary is so limited. No words can describe how I felt when facing situations like those. An illiterate person is not only deprived of her or his right of reading and writing but can't even describe their pain, which brings them a deep feeling of shame and inferiority. It is these feelings that inspired my grandma to go back to school at the age of seventy.

My grandma was frustrated with the fact that her parents had sent her brother to school but kept her home to do housework. Her parents thought that girls weren't supposed to study and that it was simply a waste of time and money that they didn't quite have back then. My grandma waited her entire life to learn to read, and it was only in her seventh decade that she wrote her name for the first time. After years of fighting illiteracy, she can now finally read the holy book. The joy in her eyes is indescribable. My grandma always tells me that if she had the opportunity to study at an early age, she would've become something—and I am sure she would've become something big. She has so much potential that got wasted just like it is the case for so many girls out there. So many potential leaders, engineers, doctors, teachers and more never came to life because they never got the chance. Instead, they are in the kitchen cooking for a husband that they once considered as their ultimate goal in life, little do they know they could've been a lot more.

I have never considered myself to be a prodigy or an exceptionally talented person. I have just worked hard all my life and was lucky enough to have a mother who knew the value of education and who supported my choices. But I recognize that not all girls around the world have the chance to access education. Some will be like my grandma and only be able to access education when they are much older. Others will never get to experience sitting in a classroom and all the joys of learning and discovering themselves that comes with it. Therefore, if you're looking at this essay and it doesn't seem like incomprehensible drawings to you, if your brain is capable of translating these letters into words and those words into meanings, know that you are extremely lucky. No matter how hard life might be and no matter how many obstacles you might face, hold on to your dreams and never give up on education. I realized the value of what I have quite early in my life, and I decided to dedicate my life and knowledge to helping others. I've used my education to find my passion and purpose. I hope that you do the same.

24

Arooj Khalid

PAKISTAN

I AM the youngest of three siblings and the only daughter in my family. From an early age, I could see that my family treated me differently from my elder brothers. My parents were exceptionally proud of my brother, a high achiever in his school; so I tried my best to follow in his footsteps. While my parents were proud of me, I felt that something was missing.

As I got older, I started asking myself questions like why am I treated differently? Why are my family's expectations from me different than those from my brothers? Why don't my brothers have to face the same pressures as I do and vice versa?

It is important to note that I didn't feel like I was treated in any way lesser than my brothers, but it was just different. As the years progressed, my curiosity about this only grew. When I shared my career aspirations, I wasn't met with the same applause and enthusiasm as my brother when he voiced similar ambitions. I was engulfed by doubt. Was it just because I was much younger than him? Or was there more to it?

As I worked through these issues around society's different expectations for girls and boys, I found solace in reading and writing. That's why, at the age of fourteen I decided that journalism was the field for me. When I declared that ambition, I was met with a muted reaction from my family. However, when I learned how to cook at the same age, I was met with way more applause and appreciation.

Despite this lacklustre response from my family, I was determined to become a journalist and raise my voice for girls everywhere. I knew that I wasn't the only one who felt differently treated. I could see many girls around me who had to face the varying effects of gender discrimination. I printed out the masthead of *The New York Times*, cut it out and pasted it on my bed board, so that it would remind me every day and night what I was supposed to do in life: raise my voice and, in turn, help girls around me find theirs.

During this time, I also had the good fortune of becoming a part of Youth Journalism International, an organization that helps young people around the world put pen to paper and speak out about local, regional and global issues. I had found them while researching opportunities to improve my writing online and applied to them right away. Through this organization, I learned how to write everything from news and feature stories to analysis and opinion pieces and explain events happening around me for an international audience. Youth Journalism International connected me to hundreds of other like-minded students worldwide, and I was able to work with them on collaborative pieces.

Youth Journalism International came into my life at a crucial point—when my country Pakistan and our education system were going through immense turmoil. Threats of violence and terrorism caused constant closure of institutions across the country, challenging our already wavering educational system. Our schools would announce closure for several days, so that they could improve their security measures. Every other week, we would hear rumours that someone had threatened to blow up our school. Not only did I witness children my age involved in rigorous full-time jobs instead of going to school, but a girl who was the same age as I was and who just wanted to go to school, was stopped and shot for doing so. Her name was Malala Yousafzai.

The violence in Pakistan continued for years to come. None of us felt safe in our schools. I still remember waking up and being scared to go to school or college because I never knew what might happen. The school administration would send out memo after memo reassuring parents that they had installed security cameras or hired more bodyguards or raised their school boundary walls. However, these efforts didn't ensure our safety. Despite the fear and insecurity, we went on with our studies. I felt that that it wasn't okay. Something had to be done, I couldn't just sit around. I needed to tell the world what was going on in my country, why it was important and why it required more attention. Youth Journalism International was the platform that came to my aid and helped me draw attention to these events. I wrote about simple things such as common traditions in Pakistan and how it felt to vote for the first time, but also about more complicated articles like interviews with child labourers and opinions on terrorism.

I was able to finish my secondary education despite school closure and security threats. By the time I graduated, the terrorism and violence had relatively subsided but it still existed in many parts of the country. I was mostly safe in a developed city and in a high-end university, but I knew that many of my compatriots weren't.

I was lucky enough to attend university after the violence had petered out. There I had many other gender-related epiphanies and shocking discoveries. I had always been in an all-girls institution before this, so with four years of co-ed study ahead, my family had a few conversations with me about what was acceptable and what wasn't. I learned that I was not supposed to 'unnecessarily' talk to my male class-fellows and should maintain a certain distance from them. At the age of nineteen, I also realized that I was now of marriageable age. Aunties at weddings would look at me in a peculiar way, now that I was all grown up and ready for marriage. I felt the pressure to hone certain skills that would probably benefit me in my married life, such as cooking.

However, all was not bleak. My university's campus was the setting of many pleasant discoveries, including the fact that there were others like me too. Being exposed to wonderful people from various cultures across Pakistan and listening to their stories helped me realize that there's so much more to life and the world that we live in than what I had been previously exposed to. I also realized that instead of feeling helpless or accepting things the way they are, we can perhaps try and change the world.

I gathered that there was so much more that I could be doing to help other girls in my community. I volunteered here and there, hoping to find a place where I could be proud of what I did. While I had the fortune of indulging in some interesting volunteer work, I was never quite satisfied. It felt like something was always missing. Sometimes the team wasn't committed to the cause, and at other times there was more exploitation of the cause rather than the actual impact being created.

Eventually, two of my friends and I got together to work on a welfare community that we called Hasaas, which means 'sensitive'. Hasaas is a group of like-minded individuals who keep finding innovative ways of using their time and efforts to minimize social inequality in Pakistan. In the beginning, most of our work was catered towards minimizing gender gap by taking small steps like conducting workshops and awareness campaigns and helping out in orphanages or shelter homes.

We used to visit village schools on the outskirts of Lahore and help the students there. While the memories are mostly sweet, one in particular stands out like a dark cloud. I remember this one time we were asked to speak about gender equity at a trust school. We created a workshop that helped girls realize their potential and learn about women in Pakistan who have broken the gender barriers and risen above stereotypes to become pilots, scientists, police officers and prime ministers of the country. It was such a rewarding Saturday. After that we sat down for tea with the principal of the school and discussed what we had achieved that day. While she was proud of her female students dreaming of travelling the world and becoming presidents and army officers, there was a hint of sadness in her eyes. She told us that most of the girls in her school drop out by the sixth grade. No matter what their dreams may be, they often have to accept and make do with the harsh realities of their life. Knowing those girls and having heard their stories and aspirations, it hit me hard. But it helped me learn an important lesson: girls are usually not in complete control of their lives and destinies. If we wanted to see the meaningful impact in girls' education, we had to change the perceptions of their teachers, parents and society as a whole.

As we tried to figure out plausible solutions to some of the barriers that students face, I found myself simultaneously fighting my own battles. I was the only girl among the three Hasaas co-founders. While my colleagues were compassionate and understanding, I have a vivid memory of feeling barred from delving into my full potential. As a girl, I did not enjoy the social mobility my male counterparts had and so there were many meetings that I had to miss, many tasks that my colleagues had to take care of without me. I would often face trouble for leaving the house more than I had to and travelling to the outskirts of the town. I was often asked, 'Out of all the girls in your university, why do YOU have to do this? '

In the junior year of my university, I received a life-changing phone call telling me I had been selected for a Global Undergraduate Scholarship that would take me to study for one semester at Michigan State University in the US. I had been working towards this scholarship for a few years. Even though it was fully funded, extended family and friends warned my parents again and again about the dangers of sending their young and unmarried daughter off to a new country all by herself. This added to my already built-up anger at the way girls are perceived in our culture, as commodities to be married off one day instead of real human beings with ambitions and dreams. Thankfully, my parents' determination and trust in me persisted, and off I went to the United States.

While I was there I learnt that owing to the selective coverage of media they were exposed to, the people in the US believed that Pakistan was a backward desert country in the Middle East. I also saw a vastly different perspective on education than the one I was used to in Pakistan. In their schools, the curriculum and pedagogy were completely different—the way their schools were structured gave students so much more freedom of thought and expression. They learnt from each other's perspectives instead of trying to blend in and become exactly alike. There are exceptions everywhere, but it seemed that the teachers there were really passionate about what they did and were actively working to improve the lives of their students through education. While I was there, I volunteered for some Montessori schools and libraries and visited a high school to speak with some of the students. I introduced my culture to young children and adults alike. The way they would ask questions and their responses to my answers helped me learn a lot about their perception and how the view of women and education differs across continents.

I used to volunteer at a children's library to read stories. One day they chose a book about one of the Supreme Court judges in the US who was a woman. While I don't remember much about it, I have a vivid memory of how I felt at that moment. The children came to the library on a Saturday and were being told a story about a woman who had faced a great deal of injustice in her life but had worked her way up to a position where she could provide justice to others. Along with my own surprise at this story, I could feel the excitement among students and especially the girls who could relate to the story of a woman facing multiple challenges in her life but persevering and succeeding. The story resonated with me, and I believe that was the moment my life took a new turn. From that point on, I started a career in education. I wanted to create content and a curriculum for children in Pakistan that exposed them to brilliant women heroes in their communities and inspired them to dream big and be passionate about those dreams.

After coming back to Pakistan, I started taking university courses in education and eventually majored in it. Throughout that time, I learnt so much from the communities I was working with and the school where I completed my student teaching experience. From my time in the classroom, it was evident that our country needs a defining and distinctive approach to fighting inequality. I deduced that improving our next generations' education could be the first step. We need to help create a culture where people, girls and boys, can question the world around them and challenge the existing norms. We need to create an environment in which they feel safe in bringing about these changes. Being in the classroom helped me understand that to fight for girls' education, we need to fight for an education that supports critical thinking and asking questions. As long as people in Pakistan are unaware of the deficiencies in the education system we currently have, they will not begin to acknowledge and recognize what needs to be fixed.

While I was on this journey, I heard about a social enterprise called Science Fuse through a friend. I saw the work that they were doing: helping children become friends with science and encouraging their sense of wonder and curiosity in a way that also complimented their culture, surroundings and communities. It was love at first sight. Luckily, Science Fuse had just opened up a call for fellowship. I didn't waste much time signing up, and I think that was one of the best decisions of my life. It felt like things were falling into place. I had found a place where I could use my skills and pursue all of my passions at once. I learned the art of science communication and started working as a volunteer. I eventually made my way up through the organization to become a Senior Project Officer. I plan, implement and monitor many of our projects, communicate with partners and stakeholders, manage teams, create the curriculum and design resources. Even today, I consider myself incredibly lucky to be a part of an organization that aligns so well with my personal goals. I am working towards encouraging girls' education and popularizing critical thinking and scientific scepticism, all together.

Not long after I started this incredible journey with Science Fuse, the world was hit by the Covid-19 pandemic. We had to switch gears quickly and I found myself doing what had inspired this whole journey in the first place: writing stories for children about Pakistani women who had faced their share of struggles but continued with their passion. Our Malala Fund-supported Science Stories project works to inspire the next generation to study science by educating them about all the amazing female scientists who came before them. Sometimes I wonder if I could go back in time to tell my younger self about these stories, what would be my reaction?

Among my many other responsibilities at Science Fuse like making DIY science videos, scripting experiments, and developing science shows and workshops for children, one of the most rewarding aspects is the engagement programme. I never thought that I would be connected to a community of hundreds of teachers across Pakistan who are as passionate and ambitious about education as I am. Even though we face many barriers in our engagements regarding gender and digital access all the time, I am grateful to have a community that is determined to find solutions and create a lasting impact. While this isn't the end of my story, it is the next chapter. From feeling powerless in the face of girls dropping out of schools to hearing parents speak about how their perception has changed and watching them help and encourage their daughters, my heart feels full and yet yearns for so much more.

25
Tina
INDIA

I LIVE in Gadiyala village of Bikaner district, which is in the western part of Rajasthan. Our ancestors have been living on this land for centuries. In the cities, people often look out for themselves instead of their neighbours; but in my region, people are there for each other. We're a warm community that respect each other.

When you look around here, you can see beautiful dunes of the Thar desert everywhere. I love this landscape. I find the dunes very calming. My family's house is located in an area that overlooks them and I never tire of looking at that view. The houses of other village folks surround our house. Some people in our community live in the dhaanis, hamlets located in the field, but we live in the village as we do not own any farming land.

My family comprises five members. My parents, two younger brothers and I. My mother is the one who keeps the house in order and manages our chores. She's also the breadwinner for our family. Through the government's Integrated Child Development Scheme, she works as an anganwadi sahayika (helper) at the anganwadi centre in our village, which is a care centre for mothers and children. She makes Rs 4,000 a month, and our family depends on that income to survive. My father is mentally challenged. He is a tailor by profession and whenever he feels better, he supports the household with his income. My favourite thing about him is how calm he is. One of my brothers is in the eighth grade and is learning stitching work in Udaipur city. My other brother is in the seventh grade. We're all very close.

In our part of the world, people often refer to girls as *paraya dhan*, which means someone else's wealth. Our society believes that a girl's life only truly begins once she marries and moves to her husband's house. Families believe a girl living in her ancestral home is merely a guest and that she's the property of her future in-laws. That's why they prioritize their son's education and don't usually invest much in their daughter's education. They don't see the point when they know that their daughter will eventually go to her husband's home and manage that house. Families are also concerned with preserving the honour of the girl so that she's an eligible future bride, which means they don't often let their daughters venture out in public spaces like schools. In families with limited means like mine, parents also marry their daughters off early to have one less mouth to feed or for the dowry. They see it as the best way for their family and their daughter to have a good life.

I'm lucky because my parents believe that education is the key to leading a good life. They have always told me that humility comes from good education and I must work hard to do well. Their passion to help me finish my schooling keeps me motivated and working hard. It's unusual to see a family like mine be supportive of girls' education. Most force their daughters to drop out. But be it homework or any emotional support, my parents are always there to help me continue my studies. My mom is always checking up on our homework and supporting us however best she can.

I believe education is the most important thing in a person's life. It's the key to your growth and development. Material wealth is temporary, but the real wealth lies in education. School is a sacred place that ensures the children are prepared to succeed in future and have good opportunities.

As I said, I come from a family with limited means. My mother was able to step up and support the household with her income only because of her educational foundation. In a society where women have to deal with such harsh unforeseeable circumstances, I worry how not completing schooling makes them highly vulnerable to more difficult situations. My friend Savitri was forced to drop out by her brother. I still feel sad that she was compelled to do that and I worry about her future.

My favourite childhood memory of school is playing on the swings in the school playground with my friend Uma. We used to have a wonderful time together in the fourth and fifth grade. I remember we used to hum songs in Marwari while playing.

My favourite subject in school is Hindi. I enjoy listening to the stories that our teacher narrates in class. Through those stories, I can travel to different locations, timelines and characters.

One of the things I look forward to after school is being a part of the Kishori Prerna Manch—an adolescent girls' groups, formed by the organization Urmul Trust. Through this group, I've also learned about good and bad touch, child rights, menstrual hygiene and other such information. I've also learned to be confident and to never doubt myself, which is not something girls in my community are taught. Due to the faith Urmul Trust has shown in me, I know now that if I have a problem, I will be able to solve it. The sense of camaraderie that they encourage all girls to develop is what makes me believe that with the right support we can do better.

As part of the group, I also got to attend a literacy festival for adolescents organized by Urmul Trust. We even had the opportunity to visit their Lunkaransar campus in Bikaner district where we interacted with so many other girls. This experience also motivated me to continue my education.

In future, I hope to become a doctor—and I know that the only way I can realize this ambition is by going to school. In my region, people are poor and they don't have access to quality health services. I have noticed that women are hesitant to get treated by a male doctor. We do not have big machines, nor do we have trained doctors. Village folk in the adjacent region pay huge bribes to get health services even in government hospitals. I want to change that. I plan to complete my medical training and then come back here to practice medicine so that everyone can access quality health care. I am motivated to come back and ensure that I do a small bit for my people.

I am currently in tenth grade. In eighth grade, I had received a B. This academic year I had hoped to perform well. However, with the Covid-19 pandemic and classes being shifted to online medium, many of us were left in the lurch. I do not have a smartphone, which made it difficult for me to keep up with the online classes. Even understanding the homework that we receive has become difficult. This year has gone by in a blur and I cannot recall a single lesson, which is very frustrating for me. I am unsure of my performance in this academic year.

However, I will not let this stop me from achieving my dream of going to school. That is also my advice to other girls. You might face barriers to your education. Your elders might not give you the support you need, your family might have a different plan for your future, a pandemic might stop you from completing your lessons for a while—but you need to fight hard. Education is the best path to the future of your choosing, whatever that may be.

Acknowledgements

DARE to Learn wouldn't have been possible without our twenty-five incredible contributors: Anjali, Anjeli, Azka Athar, Nibras Basitkey, Manisha Bharti, Vandana Bharti, Ravdanur Cuma, Houda Hamdaoui, Mungli Hasda, Shereen Kanwal, Karenjeet Kaur Bains, Arooj Khalid, Anoyara Khatun, Aramide Kayode, Husnah Kukundakwe, Aisha Mustapha, Charitie Ropati, Clarisse Alves Rezende, Katiuska Sanchez, Shweta Sharma, Rahel Sheferaw, Tamana, Tina, Angelina Tropper and Tabitha Willis. Thank you for your honesty and bravery in sharing your stories and for helping pave the way for the next generation of young leaders.

Malala Fund would also like to thank the many partners and friends who work with the contributors in this book and helped make this publication possible—including Bondita Acharya, Tabish Akhtar, National Association of Indigenous Action (ANAÍ), Abubakar Askira, Azad India Foundation, Rishita Barman, Hashima Batamuriza, Durbeen, Education for Sustainable Development (ESD), Ana Paula Ferreira De Lima, Susmita Guha, Hallmark Leadership Initiative (HALI), Yuman Hussain, Reeta Kaushik, Naval Kishor Gupta, Sreepoorna Majumdar, Srijita Majumder, Poorvi Mehrotra, Katharina Mertens-Tropper, Emebet Mulugeta, Aemiro Mussie, Raajeev Narayann, Dr. Digambar Narzary, NEDAN Foundation, Anshul Ojha, Purva Bharati Educational Trust (PBET), Ambarish Rai, Restless Development India, Right to Education Forum, Lalah Rukh Fazal-Ur-Rahman, Samudaik Kalyan Evam Vikas Sansthan (SKVS), Save the Children, Science Fuse, Prashant Singh, Aakriti Srivastava, Sangeeta Tete, Urmul Trust and Pragya Vats.

Led by Tess Thomas, this book is the product of years of hard work from the Malala Fund team—including Marielle Issa, Carine Umuhumuza, Anubhuti Patra, Bhumika Regmi, McKinley Tretler, Mahina Martinson, Noreen Plabutong, Ayesha Shakya, Chisom Onyekwere, Amanda Cosby, Lena Alfi, Julisa Tambunan, Crystal Ikanih-Musa, Moiz Hussain, Maíra Martins, Selome Taddesse, Maria Qanita, Richa Silakari, Taylor Royle and Hannah Orenstein.

About Malala Fund and Assembly

ACTIVIST and youngest Nobel laureate Malala Yousafzai began her campaign for education at the age of eleven after the Taliban took control of her town in Pakistan and banned girls from going to school. Malala spoke out publicly on behalf of other girls and their right to learn—and this made her a target.

At the age of fifteen, while returning home on the school bus, Malala was shot by the Taliban for defending girls' education. She recovered and continued her campaign to see all girls in school. With her father Ziauddin, Malala founded Malala Fund, an organization that champions every girl's right to twelve years of free, safe and quality education.

Over 130 million girls are out of school today. The reasons girls are out of school—like poverty, war and gender discrimination— differ between countries and communities. Malala Fund is working to break down the barriers that stop girls from going to school.

Malala Fund invests in education advocates in the countries with the most girls out of school. We believe local leaders are the best people to identify the problems girls face in their communities and develop solutions.

We advocate—at local, national and international levels—for resources and policy changes that girls need to go to school. Girls have high goals for themselves—and we have high expectations from leaders who can help them.

We help develop the next generation of young leaders. We believe girls should speak for themselves and tell parents, teachers and even prime ministers and presidents what they need to learn and achieve their potential. Malala Fund gives girls the tools they need to advocate for education and equality in their communities and a platform for the world to hear their voices.

This book contains twenty-five stories from Assembly, Malala Fund's award-winning digital publication and newsletter. Assembly provides girls with a platform to share their thoughts, their challenges and their accomplishments. It's a meeting place for girls around the world and a source of ideas and inspiration in their fight for education and equality. To date we've published work by girls from more than a hundred countries, translated content in twenty-six languages and reached hundreds of thousands of readers. And we would love to publish your story next.

Read more girls' stories and submit your own on assembly.malala.org

Learn more about Malala Fund's work at malala.org